WITHDRAWN

332.10973 H719w
Holland, David S.
When regulation was too
successful--the sixth

DATE DUE

When Regulation Was Too Successful—The Sixth Decade of Deposit Insurance

A History of the Troubles of the U.S. Banking Industry in the 1980s and Early 1990s

DAVID S. HOLLAND

Westport, Connecticut
London

Library of Congress Cataloging-in-Publication Data

Holland, David S.
    When regulation was too successful—the sixth decade of deposit
insurance : a history of the troubles of the U.S. banking industry
in the 1980s and early 1990s / David S. Holland.
      p. cm.
    Includes bibliographical references and index.
    ISBN 0–275–96356–X (alk. paper)
    1. Banks and banking—United States—History. 2. Deposit
insurance—United States. 3. Banks and banking—United States—
State supervision. 4. Banking law—United States—History.
I. Title.
HG2491.H64   1998
332.1′0973—dc21   98–21659

British Library Cataloguing in Publication Data is available.

Library of Congress Catalog Card Number: 98–21659
ISBN: 0–275–96356–X

First published in 1998

Praeger Publishers, 88 Post Road West, Westport, CT 06881
An imprint of Greenwood Publishing Group, Inc.

Printed in the United States of America

The paper used in this book complies with the
Permanent Paper Standard issued by the National
Information Standards Organization (Z39.48–1984).

10 9 8 7 6 5 4 3 2 1

To Rhonda

Contents

Preface

History requires the practitioner to ascertain and interpret facts. Although not easy, the first task, ascertaining facts, is relatively straightforward. In an effort such as the subject of this book, the facts are not hidden or secret. They are largely part of the public record in the archives of the media and government bodies. It is with the second task that difficulties arise. In interpreting those facts, in placing them in a perspective, the historian brings certain intellectual baggage to the table and makes subjective judgments. The underlying judgment of this book is that the disaster encountered by the savings and loan industry and the difficulties survived by the banking industry in the 1980s and early 1990s were the inevitable result of many decades of restraints on marketplace activity. The search for current culprits that occupied much of the time and effort of federal government policy-makers in both legislative and executive branches was largely misplaced. Bad guys took advantage of the situation, but the situation was the product of laws and regulations that had long since been subverted by technology and the marketplace. Others might disagree with this conclusion. I only ask that they consider the arguments with an open mind.

The intellectual baggage I brought to this effort can be attributed in large measure to many years of association and friendship with one of the more remarkable students of American banking. Carter H. Golembe has been writing about banking for almost 50 years. He has been a federal banking official, an industry consultant, and a banking director. Most importantly, he is a keen observer and perceptive analyst. His *Golembe Reports* has long been, and remains, the nation's most thought-provoking publication on the public policy aspects of banking.

Although much of my interpretation of the events of the 1980s and early 1990s is the result of my exposure to Carter's ideas and arguments, I am sure he would not agree with everything in this effort. Ultimately, this book is my own interpretation, and any errors of fact are mine. The preparation of this work for publication was done largely by my wife Rhonda, an editor and indexer of the first order.

Finally, a disclaimer. During the preparation of this book, I was on the staff of the Federal Deposit Insurance Corporation (FDIC). The interpretations, opinions, and views herein, however, were developed in my capacity as a mere taxpayer and should most certainly not be construed as those of the FDIC or any of its divisions or offices.

———

Introduction

In 1983, the Federal Deposit Insurance Corporation proudly celebrated its 50th birthday. The occasion was marked by the publication of a history of the deposit insurer's first half-century: *The Federal Deposit Insurance Corporation: The First Fifty Years*. Although low-key, the work was largely laudatory, leaving the reader with an impression of an agency characterized by quiet competence and possessed of the confidence that comes from successfully meeting difficult challenges over a long period of time.

Concerning the future, the FDIC acknowledged growing risk and instability in the banking system but predicted that the adequacy of the insurance fund and its historical relationship to the level of deposits would continue. The net worth of the insurance fund was then in excess of $15 billion, and the ratio of the fund to insured deposits was 1.22 percent. The ratio had never been below 1 percent.

Eight years later, at year-end 1991, the bank insurance fund stood at a red-ink nadir of a negative $7 billion. From year-end 1983 to year-end 1992, 1,394 banks failed, more than twice the 673 banks that had failed in the first 50 years of the FDIC's existence. Also between 1983 and 1992, the number of commercial banks fell more than 20 percent, from 14,469 institutions at year-end 1983 to 11,462 institutions at year-end 1992. The decline has continued: at year-end 1997, the number of commercial banks was 9,143, a decline of 37 percent since 1983.

What happened?

This work attempts to answer that question. The study is an examination of the banking industry's troubles of the 1980s and early 1990s, troubles that at times approached the level of a crisis. Unlike the more infamous savings and loan crisis, however, the banking troubles did not result in the decimation of an industry or a massive taxpayer bailout. The banking industry survived, and indeed today seems healthy and very much a central, fundamental component of the U.S. financial system. Nevertheless, some of the lessons that a study of the troubles could provide may not have been fully accepted. The initial government responses to the shakeout were dominated by those who believed that detailed control, regulation and supervision are the answer. Yet the underlying causes of the banking difficulties of the 1980s and early 1990s may well have been many decades of too much control, regulation, and supervision, and not enough reliance on market forces. If this contention is correct but is not the basis for legislative and regulatory oversight of the industry, banking's apparent recovery from the difficulties may not be as complete as it appears to have been, or long-lasting. Continued unwise public policies regarding the banking industry could produce, at some point in the years or decades ahead, another period of turmoil and another flirtation with the federal treasury.

Government policies and actions are the primary focus of this look at the banking troubles of the 1980s and early 1990s. The banking industry is a private sector industry and responds to many of the dynamics of the free market. But the industry was and is one of the most regulated segments of the economy. Government plays a role that is much more activist and central than is the case with the vast majority of other industries. A private sector focus for a history of the period is not impossible, but this present effort will concentrate on public policies—the activities of the Congress and government agencies.

The FDIC, the federal deposit insurance agency created in the depths of the Great Depression, was at the center of the efforts to deal with the banking troubles of the 1980s and early 1990s. Thus this study of those troubles is also a review of the FDIC's sixth, and most turbulent, decade of existence. A focus on the FDIC is further appropriate because deposit insurance, the agency's reason for being, had a causal role in the banking troubles. Deposit insurance was a major contributor to banking industry stability from the mid–1930s to the late 1970s. But as described in Chapter 1, the deposit insurance system also slowly germinated the seeds from which sprouted the difficulties of the 1980s.

Because what happened to and with the banking industry and the New Deal deposit insurer were reflections of trends and events in larger arenas, the study begins with an extended look at banking industry history and at the changing environment within which the FDIC and the other federal regulators operated. Although the banking industry is the primary focus of attention, pertinent matters concerning the remainder of the depository institutions industry, and concerning the financial industry in general, are also covered. The background material is presented in two chapters. In Chapter 1, an excess capacity interpretation of banking industry history is advanced. The argument is that what happened in the FDIC's sixth decade was in large part a consequence of a shakeout of industry excess capacity built up over a period stretching back to the nation's earliest days. Chapter 2 is an overview of the financially turbulent 1980s and the buildup to the decade.

After this look at the big picture, the focus turns to the banking industry's troubles. Chapter 3 broadly summarizes those troubles and their more notorious companion, the savings and loan (S&L) crisis. The subsequent chapters consider the banking troubles in greater detail, concentrating on several topics: too big to fail; the Texas experience; Congress's eventual acceptance that a crisis indeed existed in the S&L industry and the effects this acceptance had on banking and its regulation; the peaking of the banking problems in 1990 and 1991; and the industry's extraordinary recovery.

Finally, the government's actions during the banking troubles are assessed, and several observations on the future are offered. The government record contains both successes and failures. Unfortunately, the characterization of "successes" and "failures" is not a value-free effort, and the values or standards that one brings to the determination are not the subject of universal agreement. The basic question of how to view the survival of the banking industry and its recovery in the 1990s provides an example of the interpretation problem. Were the industry's survival and recovery a vindication of the existing regulatory structure, or did they amount to a near miss for a seriously flawed system? That question and subsidiary matters will be addressed, although definitive answers remain elusive.

The FDIC has published its own, official study of its decade of testing. As a detailed review of the decade, the study is commendable. The detail, however, can obscure several points. First, the study gives only passing attention to the deficiencies in banking industry structure that had developed as a result of many decades of close government control. These deficiencies provided the fertile ground from which sprang the troubles of depository institutions. Second, the FDIC's study acknowledges only obliquely the political battles that the troubles generated as Congress, the administration of the moment, independent agencies, and the many interested parties attempted to come to grips with what was occurring. Legislative solutions were not the products of a logical, rational process in which consensus was reached after the enlightened give-and-take of informed debate. Perhaps the FDIC's status as a government agency prevented it from describing in depth the reality of vehement disagreements, unmitigated self-interest, messy compromises, and sometimes ineffectual and sometimes excessive outcomes that constitute the legislative process. Finally, the FDIC's study spends considerable time on the techniques of bank supervision. Although important at one level, this topic can easily be accorded too much responsibility for the troubles of the decade. Would near-perfect supervision have prevented what transpired? No more than the near-perfect sand castle can withstand the ocean's waves.

THE COMPLEXITY OF REGULATION

The banking industry is not only one of the most pervasively regulated sectors of the economy; it is also subject to one of government's more complex regulatory schemes. A reader unfamiliar with that scheme might benefit from a brief—very brief—primer.

Banks are one of two types of institutions commonly referred to as depository institutions. The second type of depository institution is today called the savings association. Prior to legislation enacted in 1989—the Financial Institutions Reform, Recovery, and Enforcement Act (FIRREA)—the term most often applied to this second type of depository institution was "savings and loan association." Savings associations are also called thrifts. The use of "thrift" can sometimes be confusing, however, because the term can also encompass savings banks, one of two sub-categories of banks, the other and far larger subcategory being commercial banks. In many ways, credit unions—another type of institution—resemble banks and more especially savings associations, but credit unions are usually not included within the definition of depository institutions.

Three federal regulators share responsibility for banks. The Office of the Comptroller of the Currency (OCC), established in 1864, regulates national banks, which are generally the larger banks. The OCC is an agency in the Department of the Treasury. The independent Federal Reserve Board, established in 1913, regulates state-chartered banks that are members of the Federal Reserve System. The Federal Reserve also regulates companies that own banks. These companies are called bank holding companies. Bank and bank holding company regulation is not the principal function of the Federal Reserve Board. The principal function is the formulation and implementation of monetary policy. The independent Federal Deposit Insurance Corporation, established in 1933, insures deposits, currently for up to $100,000, in practically all banks and savings associations. The FDIC also regulates state-chartered banks that are not members of the Federal Reserve System. Because a banking organization organized in a holding company structure is regulated at both the bank level and the holding company level, it may have direct contact with more than one of the federal banking regulators. The holding company is under the supervision of the Federal Reserve, but the subsidiary bank or banks may be regulated by the OCC, the Federal Reserve, or the FDIC.

Savings associations are regulated by the Office of Thrift Supervision (OTS), which like the OCC is an agency in the Treasury Department. Prior to the enactment of FIRREA in 1989, the federal regulator of the S&L industry was the independent Federal Home Loan Bank Board, and the federal insurer for S&L deposits was its subsidiary, the Federal Savings and Loan Insurance Corporation.

Further complicating this regulatory structure is the fact that state-chartered banks and thrifts are also regulated by state regulators.

1

Excess Capacity

The troubles of the banking industry and the FDIC in the 1980s did not emerge from a void. The foundations had been laid over many decades. Indeed, what happened to the bank and thrift industries during the 1980s was a consequence of events, decisions, and developments that reached back to the nation's founding. The events, decisions, and developments produced a depository institutions industry that was, as the 1970s ended, ripe for extensive consolidation. In the language of economists, the depository institutions industry had become burdened with excess capacity. In the language of common folk, there were just too darn many banks and thrifts.

Three topics summarize the events, decisions, and developments that over the almost two centuries of the nation's existence led to excess capacity in the depository institutions industry: geographic restraints, product limitations, and deposit insurance.

GEOGRAPHIC RESTRAINTS

The geographic restraints had the longest lineage. They arose from the federal nature of the United States. Under a federal system, power is divided between the national and state governments. One of the motivations that led to the Constitutional Convention in 1787 was dissatisfaction with the impediments the newly independent states were able to impose to interstate and foreign commerce under the Articles of Confederation. Although the Constitution created a relatively strong national government and eliminated many of the state impediments to commerce, the states retained much power over economic activity.

One source of state power was the ability to license or charter business enterprises. With the exceptions of the first, 1791–1811, and second, 1816–1836, Bank of the United States, banks were among those business enterprises that required state permission to function. And again with the exceptions of the two congressionally authorized banks, few attempts to establish a bank with operations in more than one state appear to have been undertaken. The hostility of state politicians and authorities was likely one reason for the nondevelopment of interstate banking organizations. Probably at least as important, however, was that the optimum bank size—the use of the term implies a broad, ill-defined range rather than a precise point—in the first half of the nineteenth century was not large. That optimum size increased with improvements in transportation, communications, and organizational capabilities, but the increase was slow and incremental. Banks developed as small, local organizations, and very few "natural" banking markets were hampered by state boundaries. Banking services over distances were provided through various types of correspondent relationships.

Thus the role of state governments in authorizing and controlling economic activities combined with the narrow geographic service areas of early banks to make state boundaries the outermost limits of banks' physical presences. This situation was further solidified when the national banking system came into being during the Civil War. The national banking system checked the growth of branch banking and consequently hindered the development of one important means by which banks could have expanded their service areas.

Branch banking was fairly common before the Civil War. The first and second Bank of the United States both had multiple, interstate facilities. The first Bank had 8 branches, and the second Bank had 25 branches. Within states, state-authorized banks had varying degrees of branching powers. Branch banking was particularly common in the South and the West. According to one compilation, 27 banks in 14 states in 1848 had a total of 143 branches. In 1860, 39 banks in 13 states had 222 branches.[1] The laws that brought the national banking system into existence, however—the National Currency Act of 1863 and the National Bank Act of 1864—did not provide for branch banking. And the initial attitude of the new agency, the Office of the Comptroller of the Currency, overseeing national banks was not favorable toward branching. Most of the state banks with branches that converted to the new national charters became single office institutions. Not only did interest in branch banking wane, opposition to the concept became widespread. Nevertheless, a number of states still permitted their state-chartered banks to have multiple offices.

Not until the end of the century was interest rekindled, in part due to a dearth of banking services in small communities, and not until the 1920s did economic pressure for more banking facilities became pronounced. The inability of national banks to branch put them at an increasing disadvantage to state-chartered institutions. In 1927, Congress through the McFadden Act allowed national banks to branch within cities to the same extent as could state banks. The branching power was expanded in the Banking Act of 1933 to permit branching by national banks throughout a state to the same extent as state authorities permitted branching by state banks. But branching still had its opponents. Indeed, one of the motivations for the establishment of federal deposit insurance in other provisions of the 1933 act was a desire to strengthen the banking system through an alternative other than widespread branching, which many believed would threaten the thousands of local, community banks.[2]

In the decades following passage of the 1933 act, most states slowly relaxed their branching rules. Unit banking gave way to some degree of branching; restrictive branching gave way to branching over wider areas or statewide. Until very recently, however, state boundaries remained as ultimate barriers to bank branching.

Another means of geographic expansion—both within states with restrictive branching laws and interstate—began attracting interest in the early 1950s. A few organizations turned to the holding company structure as a means of engaging in activities not permitted banks and of establishing banking offices beyond the barriers erected by branching laws. In 1956, the Bank Holding Company Act put limits on the potential of holding companies. The product limitations are noted shortly. Regarding geographic limitations, the Douglas Amendment to the Act prohibited ownership of banks by out-of-state holding companies unless this ownership was specifically permitted by state law. Until the 1980s, few states had such laws.

The consequence of this long history of geographic restrictions on banking operations was an industry organized along, and both protected and constrained by, political boundaries, notably state lines but also in many instances city and county limits. How did these geographic restrictions affect industry structure? The answer, of course, requires a fair degree of speculation. But it is certainly logical to argue that in the absence of the pervasive influence of state and local boundaries, the banking industry would have developed in a much more concentrated direction. Fewer banks would likely have been established. The number of banking offices—banks and branches—might not have been substantially different, but the number of independent banks would probably have been much lower.

A more concentrated banking industry, with fewer banks, would not necessarily have resulted in a less competitive industry. Indeed, the geographic barriers to bank activities most likely produced a lower overall level of competition in the industry than otherwise would have been the case. Banks in many areas were protected from the full rigors of a competitive marketplace. Because of the geographic restrictions, the nation very probably ended up with more banks than would have existed in a competitively unfettered environment.

Ironically, the anticompetitive effects of geographic restrictions—and to a lesser extent product limitations—were probably exacerbated by enthusiastic enforcement of the antitrust laws. In the 1960s, 1970s, and early 1980s, even a modicum of overlap in the markets of banks desiring to combine would provoke a substantial antitrust challenge. The result was another limitation on the ability of banks to grow. Laws restricting geographic expansion limited the ability of banks to expand beyond their existing geographic markets, and antitrust laws limited the ability of banks to grow by merger within their markets. Thus as technology and the marketplace were raising the optimum size for an organization providing banking services, artificial constraints were severely hampering the ability of banks to respond. Further restricting the ability of banks to grow were state and federal requirements, enforced with varying degrees of vigor at different times, that new branches be justified by a showing of need in the community. Such a showing was more difficult if the area was being served by another bank or branch. Consequently, a bank could be doubly stymied: it could not acquire the other bank because of the alleged reduction in competition, and it could not open a competing branch because the increase in competition was allegedly not warranted.

PRODUCT LIMITATIONS

Product limitations had less clear origins and less certain effects than did geographic restraints. Varying interpretations of the historical record regarding such limitations have been offered. The interpretation suggested herein is that what began as legal buttressing of normal economic specialization gradually became legal impediments to meeting the changes of normal economic growth and development. The result was a financial industry with an excessive number of service and product providers.

The relationship between the government and private sectors for much of U.S. history prior to the New Deal years is sometimes described by the term laissez-faire. Governments allegedly left businesses largely alone, and the latter functioned, developed, and changed according to the dictates of the marketplace. This simplistic situation, however, was never fully the case. Governments, particularly state governments, were involved in a variety of ways in the business world. A few private sector endeavors, some toll roads, for example, received affirmative government backing in the form of monopolies and even outright monetary support. A far greater number of commercial and financial enterprises were dependent on government for charters and licenses under which to operate.

In the early years of the development of commerce and finance, these charters and licenses generally matched the contemplated business with the marketplace. The fit may not have always been precise, but it usually was fairly close. The law—the charters, licenses, and statutes that standardized the procedure—took its cue from how economic life functioned and what economic life demanded. At some ill-defined point, however, the tail began to wag the dog. The charters and licenses did not just reflect the needs of the marketplace, they also shaped and directed how the marketplace developed. As economic life became more complex, as specialization increased, change was channeled by the charters, licenses, and statutes of earlier, simpler times. In some cases, this channeling might have followed natural economic courses. In other cases, however, the channels might have become more like canals, forcing economic development in directions it would not have otherwise gone.

This interpretation of the flow of U.S. economic history might be particularly apt in the field of finance. Banking and insurance were, and are, businesses narrowly defined. Initially, the narrowness was contained in charters granted by legislatures for individual institutions. Later, when states adopted laws, such as the free banking laws, permitting the more widespread formation of financial institutions, the narrowness was set forth in statutes.[3] Financial specialization became codified in enactments of state legislatures. Banks, building and loan associations, credit unions, trust companies, life insurance companies, property and casualty insurance companies—these and other types of financial institutions were given narrow product markets in which to operate. Specialization also resulted from attempts to correct perceived abuses, actual or potential. For example, the Glass-Steagall Act of 1933, which partially separated commercial and investment banking, was a response to what were thought at the time to be widespread abuses in the underwriting, distribution, and sale of securities. These abuses in turn were thought to be a significant contributor to the banking and economic problems of the early 1930s. The Bank Holding Company Act of 1956 and the Bank Holding Company Act Amendments of 1970, which among other things made the combination of banking and other financial businesses subject to approval and scrutiny by the Federal Reserve Board, were enacted in part to prevent the development of financial conglomerates with their supposedly attendant undue concentrations of power and conflicts of interest.

Legally mandated financial specialization not only limited the products that financial organizations could offer; equally as important, it created markets protected by law from many competitive influences. Participants and customers benefitting from the situation constituted politically powerful interest groups that made changes in the government-mandated specialization exceedingly difficult. Over the longterm, legally mandated financial specialization hindered marketplace-driven changes in the financial industry, restricted the ability of institutions to offer new products and services, and prolonged the life of inefficient organizations. As technology and the marketplace evolved, legal product limitations became more confining. In short, legally mandated financial specialization contributed to the development of banking, insurance, and securities as separate industries, resulting in more players in the financial arena than would have otherwise been the case.

A DIGRESSION—BANKING AND COMMERCE

In recent decades, a part of the debate over product limitations has involved a banking-commerce controversy. The issue is whether banking and commerce—"commerce" meaning not other financial businesses such as insurance and securities but nonfinancial businesses—should be allowed to intermingle. In the search for support for their respective positions, proponents of the different sides of the controversy have turned to history. One side has argued, frequently from a review of statutes, charters, and other legal documents, that banking and commerce have been strictly separated throughout much of the nation's existence.[4] The other side has found considerable evidence of substantial and long term intermingling.[5] A digression into this controversy might be helpful in illuminating the complexities of the topic of product limitations and in supporting the assertion that over the years these limitations have become more confining.

Searchers of the historical record in the banking-commerce controversy often have become sidetracked. One false path has been a focus on activities rather than on ownership. The questions investigated have included: Have both banking and commercial functions been performed in the same entity? At any point in the nation's history, have banks been significantly engaged in commercial activities? Have commercial enterprises also functioned as banks?

The answers to these questions are obscured by the way business was organized and conducted in much of the nineteenth century. Unrelated activities in a single entity were the exception. As with the complexity of many aspects of social, political, and economic life, complexity in the internal organization and functions of business enterprises has increased considerably over the 200 years of the nation's existence. Thus searching for examples of multiple businesses being performed within a single entity in the nation's early years is not likely to be a productive endeavor.

A more appropriate historical focus than activities within a single enterprise is common ownership of businesses engaged in unrelated or only semirelated activities. And at least as significant as common ownership are interlocking directories as ways of binding businesses together. When these topics are investigated, the historical record becomes much more varied. Particularly in the latter part of the nineteenth century, common ownerships and interlocking directories were frequently found.[6] Indeed, the so-called Money Trust was alleged to control much of American industry at the turn of the century. This small group of bankers, most prominently J. Pierpoint Morgan, owed its power to directorships, voting trustees, stock holdings, and of course access to funds. Hostility to the Money Trust was an important political force in the early twentieth century, and the Trust's power was the subject of one of the more famous congressional investigations in U.S. history, the Pujo Committee hearings in 1912. Concern about the Money Trust helped produce several major laws, including the Federal Reserve Act of 1913.

Exactly how organized and conspiratorial the Money Trust was is still subject to debate. What is clear, however, is that in the latter decades of the nineteenth century and the first decade or so of the twentieth century, a significant degree of common control existed between banking and commerce. A relatively small group of bankers was the principal source of funds for large-scale commercial ventures. The funds came from both the bankers themselves and from investors who relied on the bankers for advice. And through corporate boards and voting trusts, the bankers had significant says in the policies of, and ready access to information on, commercial enterprises. One historian has characterized the U.S. economy in the half century before World War I as being "financier-centered" and credits the small group of powerful financiers with channeling the capital that produced growth in the important industries of the time: railroads, steel, electricity, and telephones.[7]

The close relationship between banking and commerce that existed in turn-of-the-century America—a relationship bordering in many instances on common control—began changing shortly before and during World War I. To ward off legally mandated divestitures of their cross-holdings, the Money Trusters curtailed some of their activities. The large borrowings by the national government during the war significantly expanded the securities distribution business. A sizeable proportion of the new government bonds went to the common man, and firms handling this retail bond distribution for the government grew. After the war, a 10-year stock market boom further increased consumer interest in the securities business.

In 1933, the Glass-Steagall Act, enacted in response to perceived causes of the stock market crash of 1929 and the subsequent Great Depression, largely separated the commercial and investment banking businesses. By separating the two, the act reduced the power of each, and the combined power of both, regarding nonbanking sectors of the economy. Segmentation of banking dispersed power over a greater number of entities, thus diluting the ability to exert control. Power dispersion and power reduction go hand-in-hand. After World War II, the growth in the retail securities business and the several-decades-long economic expansion further eroded the combined power of the now separate banking and securities industries. The growth in the retail securities business, and in securities ownership, continued the dispersion of the power that arose from the ability to provide or channel funds. In addition, the long economic expansion, stretching with only minor interruptions from 1945 to 1973, enabled corporations to look inward for financing: the reinvestment of profits met a substantial proportion of the fund needs of many enterprises. Finally, the Bank Holding Company Act of 1956 and the Bank Holding Company Act Amendments of 1970 came close to enshrining as national policy the separation of commercial banks and commercial organizations.

Thus, over much of the twentieth century a retreat has been underway from the high point of common control in banking and commerce that existed in the Money Trust's heyday. The retreat has not been a rout. In part as a result of affiliations among corporate boards of directors, a significant degree of influence between banking and commerce is prevalent today. Bankers sit on the boards of commercial enterprises, and businessmen sit on the boards of banks. Still, partly as a result of legal mandates, banking-commerce affiliations are not as pervasive today as they appear to have been a century ago.

The point to be gleaned from this digression into the banking-commerce controversy is that at least at the ownership level, a rigid separation of banking and commerce has not been the norm in U.S. economic history. The trend regarding banking-commerce affiliations has been toward more legal restrictions. This trend in the direction of the law appears to be opposite to trends fostered by technology and the marketplace that are breaking down economic barriers separating the development and marketing of divergent products and services. The growing legal separation of banking and commerce most likely has not been as economically harmful—has not been anywhere near as great a producer of excess capacity—as have product limitations within the financial industry itself. But the legal reinforcements of the separation are the result of a mind-set that has tended to look at products and services individually and on a stand-alone basis. Such a mind-set produced the product limitations in the financial industry that in turn contributed to the growth over many decades of the industry's excess capacity.

DEPOSIT INSURANCE

The third factor that together with geographic restraints and product limitations resulted in excess capacity in the banking industry was deposit insurance. Federal deposit insurance, the FDIC's raison d'être, was one of the major New Deal initiatives to forestall future financial crises. At the state level, deposit insurance experiments dated back to 1829, although all had been abandoned by 1933. Calls for federal deposit insurance were common in the latter part of the nineteenth century and the early years of the twentieth century. Between 1886 and 1933, 150 deposit insurance or guaranty proposals were put before the Congress.[8] It took the trauma of the onset of the Great Depression, however, and the failure of approximately 9,000 banks between 1929 and 1933 for federal deposit insurance to become law. Moreover, the desirability of federal deposit insurance as a response to the banking industry troubles was not universally accepted. President Franklin Roosevelt, the American Bankers Association, and the Office of the Comptroller of the Currency were among the opponents.[9] Some saw deposit insurance as perpetuating an inherently unsafe banking structure grounded on many thousands of small banks exposed to the vicissitudes of local economic conditions. Others were concerned about the potential costs of the federal guarantee.

But federal deposit insurance became law and by one set of measures was spectacularly successful. Since the inception of the program, no insured deposits have been lost. Moreover, for 50 years, until the early 1980s, the nation's banking industry was extraordinarily stable. Bank runs, the bane and fear of pre–1933 banking, were practically nonexistent. And for much of the period, from 1943 through 1981, the number of failures was close to infinitesimal. During those years, the number of failed banks equaled or exceeded 10 only four times—13 in 1975, 16 in 1976, and 10 each in 1980 and 1981—and was actually zero in one year, 1962, a nonevent much touted by the FDIC, which attributed the achievement to generally favorable economic conditions, progressive and alert bank management, the effectiveness of bank supervisors, and the confidence of bank depositors resulting from deposit insurance.[10] To put these figures in perspective, the number of banks during the period never fell below 13,000.

But the success of deposit insurance was deceptive. The fact that no insured deposits were lost fulfilled one of the goals of deposit insurance. But the separate and distinct fact that the number of bank failures was small was not necessarily an unmitigated good. Government regulators, Congress, and the general public certainly seemed pleased with the situation, but the lack of failures could also be viewed as an indication of an overly protected industry, one in which normal market forces were not allowed to cull the inefficient and the excess. In short, for half a century practically no exits from the banking industry occurred.

Why the federal deposit insurance program fostered a regulatory attitude that was adverse to even the tiniest bit of industry attrition probably was due to human nature. Perhaps as a regulator and supervisor of banks, the FDIC naturally came to view them protectively. Perhaps the long-standing widespread desire to provide and maintain banking services in even the smallest communities produced a bias against actually closing banking facilities. Whatever the cause, within a short time of the FDIC's inception, the focus of the agency's attention, and indeed the attention of most public policy practitioners, had gone beyond the protection of insured depositors to the protection of banks themselves. The shift was largely unnoticed. One set of consequences of the regulatory focus on banks themselves was that the banking business became governed by pervasive rules and regulations and closely monitored by bank examiners. A bank failure became an extremely difficult thing to engineer, at least in "normal" times.

The aversion to closing banking facilities not only produced excess banking capacity in its own right, the attitude also contributed to an environment in which the development of excess capacity was extremely likely. Depositors and other creditors had little fear of loss. Insured deposits were backed, implicitly, by the federal government. And the fact that very few banks were liquidated meant that uninsured deposits and other liabilities were subject to minimal risk. Consequently, depositors and other creditors had little incentive to monitor the conditions of banks, and little apprehension about placing funds in the banking system.

For their part, bankers were constrained primarily by laws, regulations, and the regulators. The normal restraints of the marketplace were much diminished. Funds were readily available to banks, more so as the 1960s gave way to the 1970s, and the 1970s became the 1980s. As the conditions that produced the financial conservatism of the immediate post-Great Depression years receded from memory, bankers became less skeptical and wary, and more willing to court risk. At the extreme, the concept of "moral hazard" took over. Managers, and in some cases owners, of depository institutions had little to lose and possibly much to gain from risk-embracing behavior.

CONCLUSION

The result of geographic restrictions, product limitations, and deposit insurance was the development over many decades of excess capacity in the depository institutions industry. Proof for this assertion is elusive because measuring excess capacity in an industry in which the products are mostly intangible is difficult. In part, the assertion is intuitive: factors that limit and protect markets—geographic restrictions and product limitations—and that reduce the likelihood of failure—deposit insurance—would seem inevitably to lead to more industry participants than would otherwise be the case.

After-the-fact evidence—ex post in the jargon of economists—also exists for the assertion that excess capacity existed. The fact that in the 9-year period from year-end 1983 to year-end 1992 more than twice the number of banks failed, 1,394, as failed in the preceding 50 years supports the conclusion that too many banks existed in 1983. When mergers and other consolidations are taken into account, the reduction in the number of commercial banks is even more striking. The number of banks fell more than 20 percent over the period, from 14,469 at year-end 1983 to 11,462 at the year-end 1992. At year-end 1997, the number of commercial banks was 9,143, a decline of 37 percent since 1983.[11] For the 10 years from year-end 1984 to year-end 1997, the number of independent banking organizations—bank holding companies plus unaffiliated banks and thrifts—fell 40 percent, from 14,888 to 8,967.[12]

Parenthetically, a similar episode of banking industry consolidation can be also interpreted as a shakeout of excess capacity. From 1925 through 1933, the number of banks declined from 29,052 to 14,771.[13] Much of the decline occurred after the onslaught of the Great Depression—the number of banks at year-end 1929 was 25,568—and a variety of factors led to this economic catastrophe. But an excess capacity view of the U.S. financial industry as the Depression commenced has some appeal. The mere fact that the number of banks declined by almost 50 percent is itself evidence of too many credit providers. Moreover, financial speculation characterized the last half of the 1920s, and financial speculation requires at least an ample supply of credit. Where the availability of credit is excessive, financial speculation is a distinct possibility. Consequently, financial speculation is also evidence of too many credit providers.

Excess capacity in finance is not just a question of too many brick-and-mortar facilities. The matter is considerably more complicated. The intangible nature of the products of the banking and financial industries renders the physical facilities of those industries little more than indications of the ability to create and provide financial goods and services. At one of its broadest meanings in regard to the financial industry, the term "excess capacity" encompasses the power to create credit. In a financially advanced economy with many financial intermediaries and many possible paths for the flow of funds, credit creation power is widespread and takes many forms. Where laws such as those mandating geographic restrictions, product limitations, and deposit insurance result in greater numbers of participants in the financial field than might otherwise be the case, it seems logical to conclude that the power to create credit can become excessive. Supply exceeds demand. Unfortunately, getting a handle on an economy's ability to create financial goods and services, including credit, is not an easy task. In the absence of quantitative measurements of more direct indicators, numbers of financial institutions serve as a very imperfect proxy for financial capacity.

Studies of excess capacity in the banking and financial industries have been few. Often the assertion is made that excess capacity exists or existed, but little supporting evidence or analysis is given. For example, the commission created by Congress to study the thrift crisis buried a reference to excess capacity in its report: "If over-capacity in the S&L industry had been eliminated in the late 1960s and 1970s, a smaller, leaner and more profitable industry would have been more resilient to the huge shocks that occurred during the great credit crunch."[14]

A preliminary study released by the staff of the New York Federal Reserve Bank in 1993 is an exception to the general lack of analysis of excess capacity in the financial industry.[15] The study, which focused on recent history, found that an excess capacity problem emerged in the banking industry in the 1980s. The emergence was attributed to a variety of factors, including: (1) the rise of new competitors such as foreign banks, finance companies, pension funds, and mutual funds; (2) a reduction in the proportion of household assets entrusted to banks in the form of deposits;[16] and (3) a volatile economic environment that produced high rates of business failures and relatively low rates of net business formations, conditions not favorable for banking profitability. The emphasis in the study was on the 1980s and the logic was a little hard to follow, but a possible long term reason for the development of excess capacity was suggested that made more intuitive sense: the pervasive regulatory structure surrounding banking and the difficulty of exiting the industry.

To summarize this chapter, an excess capacity interpretation of the history of the U.S. financial industry, primarily the banking sector thereof, has been presented.

The assertion is that geographic restrictions, product limitations, and federal deposit insurance produced a banking industry with an ability to create more financial products, principally credit, than the economy could safely absorb. In short, the banking industry had too many providers of goods and services. By the beginning of the 1980s, the capacity overhang had been growing without interruption for 50 years. The overhang helped usher in a decade of financial turmoil.

NOTES

1.   John M. Chapman and Ray B. Westerfield, *Branch Banking: Its Historical and Theoretical Position in America and Abroad* (New York: Harper & Brothers Publishers, 1942), p. 3.

2.   Ross M. Robertson, updated by Jesse M. Stiller, *The Comptroller and Bank Supervision*, 2nd ed. (Washington, D.C.: Office of the Comptroller of the Currency, 1995), p. 184; Carter H. Golembe, "The Deposit Insurance Legislation of 1933," *Political Science Quarterly* (June 1960, Vol. 67), pp. 195–99.

3.   The first free banking law was adopted by the State of New York in 1838.

4.   See, for example, Melanie L. Fein and M. Michele Faber, "The Separation of Banking and Commerce in American Banking History," an Appendix to a Statement by Federal Reserve Board Chairman Paul Volcker before a subcommittee of the House Committee on Government Operations, June 11, 1986; E. Gerald Corrigan, "The Banking-Commerce Controversy Revisited," *Quarterly Review*, Federal Reserve Bank of New York (Spring 1991, Vol. 16/1), pp. 1–13.

5.   See, for example, Carter H. Golembe, "'Hold That Line'—The Federal Reserve Board's View of the Banking Business," *Golembe Reports* (Vol. 1986–8); Carter H. Golembe, "A Thanksgiving Basket—Mr. Boesky; FDIC/FSLIC; the Number of Commercial Banks; Banking and Commerce Revisited," *Golembe Reports* (Vol. 1986–10); J. Bradford De Long, "What Morgan Wrought," *The Wilson Quarterly* (Autumn 1992), pp. 17–30.

6.   Common ownership could, and can, take several forms. Probably the most frequently found in early U.S. history is ownership by an individual or a group of two or more enterprises. The group could be organized in a number of ways, including a partnership, stockholders acting in concert, or a holding company or its equivalent. Common ownership, as used herein, also refers to the ownership of one business by another. For example, a commercial enterprise could own a bank, or a bank could own a commercial enterprise. Neither situation is unprecedented. See Loretta J. Mester, "Banking and Commerce: A Dangerous Liaison?" *Business Review*, Federal Reserve Bank of Philadelphia (May–June 1992), p. 18.

7.   De Long, p. 26.

8.   Golembe, "Deposit Insurance Legislation," p. 188.

9.   Robertson.

10.   Federal Deposit Insurance Corporation, *Annual Report, 1962*, p. 4.

11.   FDIC, *Annual Reports*, individual years; *Historical Statistics on Banking, 1934–1992*; *Statistics on Banking*, individual years.

12.   FDIC, *Quarterly Banking Profile, Graph Book* (4th quarter, 1997).

13.   U.S. Department of Commerce, *Historical Statistics of the United States, Colonial Times to 1970* (Washington, D.C.: U.S. Government Printing Office), p. 1019.

14.   National Commission on Financial Institution Reform, Recovery and Enforcement, *Origins and Causes of the S&L Debacle: A Blueprint for Reform* (Washington, D.C., July 1993), p. 31.

15. Federal Reserve Bank of New York, *Studies on Excess Capacity in the Financial Sector* (June 1993).

16. The relationship between a reduction in the proportion of household assets entrusted to the banking industry and excess capacity may not be readily apparent. Would not a reduction in the raw material of banking—deposits—automatically produce a shrinkage in the industry? Probably so over the long term. For the short term, however, the infrastructure—personnel and facilities—to support the intermediation of a certain proportion of household assets is perhaps not so easily shed.

2

A Turbulent Time

What social and cultural turbulence were to the 1960s, financial turbulence was to the 1980s. In the world of money, the decade was a volatile, exuberant period, and depository institutions—banks and savings and loans—partook of their fair share of the good life and suffered their fair share of the upheavals. This chapter details the buildup to the 1980s and suggests several broad themes that characterize the decade. In the next chapter, the focus is narrowed to depository institutions in the 1980s.

THE BUILDUP

A snapshot at any point in time is really a picture of the cumulative results of all that has gone before. The connections between some present conditions and past situations are readily discernable. In other instances, the cause and effect relationships are much less clear. But in all cases, the present cannot properly be considered in isolation from the past. Regarding depository institutions, one important legacy of the past was discussed in the first chapter—excess capacity. In this section of Chapter 2, the years leading up to the 1980s are considered in more detail. Trends and events of those years helped produce the turmoil that followed.

World War II is often a starting point for histories of the recent past, including the recent financial and economic past. The war ended with a well–defined situation: an economically supreme United States, the remainder of the industrial world *in extremis*, and the potential of the nonindustrialized world apparent to only a few. Although it was not the intent, the Bretton Woods Conference of 1944 had implicitly anointed the U.S. dollar as the lynchpin of the international financial order, an anointment that worked because it comported with economic reality.

The world has never been static, however, and the balance of financial and economic power was bound to undergo movement as the years passed. These changes in the international environment both brought about and were effected by changes in the U.S. domestic economy. Parenthetically, it is worth noting that the existence of the relationships between the international economic environment and the U.S. domestic economy was not accepted by many Americans. Indeed, a fair number of the citizens of the United States still refuse today to accept the fact that the U.S. economy is a part of the larger world economy.

One significant change was the inevitable economic recovery of Western Europe—particularly Germany—and Japan. With educated, trained, productive populations, at least a modicum of belief in the decisions of the marketplace, access to raw materials, and the jumpstart of U.S. financial aid, the prewar industrialized nations had nowhere to go but up. And because so much of their infrastructure had been destroyed, the upward journey was also a modernization voyage. A result was that by the 1960s the U. S. hegemony was being challenged. International flows of goods, services, and funds were taking new paths, creating consternation and causing disruptions among those accustomed to the old routes.

The paramount position of the U.S. dollar was one victim of the changing economic relationships. As the economies of other countries surged relative to the economy of the United States, the belief in the dollar as the stable foundation of the international financial system faded. Overseas holders of dollars worried about potential losses in the value of their holdings. Ups and downs in the U.S. economy caused ripples in the international money markets. Periodic crises of confidence in the dollar led to much jetting across the oceans and numerous international conferences and meetings, which occasionally produced agreements purporting to solve the perceived problem of the moment. The solutions, however, turned out to be no more than temporary.

One set of contributors to the dollar's problems was loose monetary and fiscal policies in the United States during the mid– and late–1960s as the nation tried to fund both the Vietnam War and a massive growth in social welfare programs without incurring any financial hardships, such as increased taxes. The loose monetary and fiscal policies started an inflationary spiral that was to be an important precipitant of the depository institution problems of the 1980s.

In the early 1970s, the declining fortunes of the dollar finally produced the demise of the dollar-based fixed-exchange rate system that had evolved from the Bretton Woods Conference of 1944. The fixed-exchange rate system was replaced by a modified floating exchange rate system in which the major currencies were allowed to fluctuate against one another. One consequence was an enormous growth in currency trading and related activities in the banking industry. This growth in turn helped foster a general environment of change and innovation.

Another consequence was the removal of a possible restraint on the inflationary spiral that was getting under way. Inflation under a fixed-rate regime often quickly leads to pressure on a currency that in turn spurs the government to adopt non-inflationary policies. Under a flexible-rate regime, on the other hand, depreciation of the currency can preclude, or at least postpone, the need to bite the bullet with tight monetary and fiscal policies. A government is often willing to tolerate currency depreciation as the lesser of two evils.

In 1973, the incipient inflationary spiral received a king-size boost. The oil-exporting countries, operating through their cartel the Organization of Petroleum Exporting Countries (OPEC), imposed a fourfold increase in the price of oil. Additional increases followed as the decade progressed. The increase in the price of a basic commodity caused an upward ratcheting of prices throughout the economy. Inflation and interest rates reflected the climb.

For example, the largest annual increase in the consumer price index (CPI) in the 1960s had been 5.5 percent in 1969. During 1974, the first full year after the initial oil-price boost, the CPI rose 11 percent. The annual increase fell to 5.8 percent in 1976 but returned to double digits by the end of the decade. For 1979, 1980, and 1981, the CPI increases were 11.3 percent, 13.5 percent, and 10.3 percent, respectively.[1]

Regarding interest rates, the annual rate on new issues of three–month U.S. Treasury securities reached 10.0 percent in 1979, its first ever foray into double digits. The yield on new-home mortgages went from 7.7 percent in 1971 to 10.8 percent in 1979, 14.7 percent in 1981, and 15.1 percent in 1982. The prime rate charged by banks hit 18.9 percent in 1981; in 1971 it had been 5.7 percent.[2]

In October 1979, the increasing inflation and interest rates spurred Paul Volcker's Federal Reserve Board to abandon the direct targeting of interest rates. The new primary target was the money supply. The theory was that over the long term a slow steady growth in the money supply would result in only modest levels of inflation. The long term, however, would take time to arrive. Meanwhile, interest and inflation rates continued climbing.

As the economic environment was undergoing these profound changes, technology was adding its bit of uncertainty to the financial arena. Computers and computerized communications were making credit, market, and product information more accessible. The delivery of financial services was becoming less dependent on customer or institution location. Technology was contributing to the assault on the competitive barriers—the geographic and product restraints discussed in Chapter 1 —that had long protected the franchises of banks and S&Ls.

Thus the 1970s were years of increasing volatility in the banking world. The international financial order was rapidly changing. Interest rates, at the time the major determinant of revenues and expenses for depository institutions—and still a principal factor today—were entering uncharted territory. The onrush of the information age was altering how financial products and services were developed and delivered. Those comfortable with the way banking had been done for decades were becoming uneasy, at least those prescient enough to realize that the foundations of their world were crumbling. Those with an entrepreneurial bent were eagerly analyzing the changing landscape for potentially profitable opportunities.

By the end of the decade, the changing world had produced significant inroads in the traditional franchises of depository institutions. On the asset side—the lending side—of the balance sheet, banks encountered increased competition from finance companies, the commercial paper market, and foreign sources of funds. The statistics do not fully reflect the extent of the competition. For example, between 1970 and 1980, bank loans as a percentage of the total liabilities of corporate businesses declined only a little over two percentage points, from 18.8 percent to 16.7 percent.

The finance company share of the corporate business market increased from 1.98 percent to 3.22 percent, the commercial paper market share from 1.30 percent to 2.04 percent, and the foreign direct investment share from 2.02 percent to 8.01 percent.[3]

What the relatively small decline in the bank share of the corporate lending market masks is that the banking industry's competitors were making a good proportion of their gains in the quality end of the market. Only the soundest corporations could issue commercial paper, for example. Thus the increased competition encountered by banks during the decade was very noticeable because it was for their best customers.

On the liabilities side—the deposit-taking side—of the balance sheet, the interplay between the high interest rates and the interest rate ceilings on banks and S&Ls produced a new competitor almost from scratch. That competitor was the money market mutual fund industry.

Interest rate ceilings were a legacy of the Great Depression. In the early 1930s, one popular explanation—since substantially discredited—for the troubles was the payment of excessive interest on deposits. As a result, the authority to promulgate interest rate ceilings for time and savings deposits for banks was contained in the Banking Acts of 1933 and 1935.[4] It was three decades, however, before market interest rates began bumping up against the ceilings. In 1957, in response to increased business loan demand, increased competition for funds, and rising rates, the interest rate ceilings were raised for the first time. Four more increases came in the early 1960s.

In 1966, the ceilings were expanded to include S&Ls, which were having trouble competing with banks for funds in the gradually more volatile interest rate environment. Because the essence of their business was the funding of long-range assets with short term liabilities, S&Ls were not as able as banks to move quickly to higher rates. Indeed, higher rates were a real threat to S&L profitability. The interest income from the long-range assets rose much more slowly than the interest expense on the short term deposits. Congress instructed the banking agencies and the S&L regulator, the Federal Home Loan Bank Board, to coordinate their decisions on ceilings. In implementing the expanded ceilings structure, the regulators established a differential for S&Ls. The S&L ceilings were higher than the bank ceilings, which was hoped would aid in keeping an adequate supply of funds flowing to the housing markets.

Market interest rates continued to increase in volatility and to reach new heights. In 1966, 1969–70, 1973–74, and 1978–80, the ceilings prevented depository institutions from fully meeting the rates available elsewhere. One of those "elsewheres" was a new animal, the money market mutual fund.

Money market mutual funds, or money market funds (MMFs) for short, are mutual funds that limit their investments to short term money market instruments. Originated by securities firms and mutual fund groups, MMFs were beyond the reach of much banking industry legislation, including the laws and regulations on deposit interest rate ceilings. Many MMFs could be redeemed by drafts, thus giving them the appearance of interest-bearing checking accounts. The first MMF appeared in 1972, and 50 were in existence by the end of 1977, but net assets were less than $4 billion.[5] The period of exponential growth commenced with the interest rate upsurge that began in 1978. At the end of February 1980, 79 MMFs with total assets in excess of $60 billion were in existence.

By the late 1970s, competition from the MMFs was posing a significant threat to the banking and S&L industries. High interest rates seemed to have become firmly entrenched. The interest rate ceilings prevented banks and S&Ls from meeting the interest rates of the marketplace. With much reluctance, Congress responded to the situation by providing for the phasing out of the interest rate ceilings. The law was the Depository Institutions Deregulation and Monetary Control Act of 1980. Although myopically opposed by a sizeable number of bank and, especially, S&L industry executives, the interest rate ceiling phaseout was almost a necessity for the industries' continued existence. The nitty-gritty of the matter was that depository institutions were subject to cost controls while their growing number of competitors were not, an untenable state of affairs for long term survival.

Nevertheless, although almost a necessity, the phasing out of interest rate ceilings was a traumatic move. The previously slow wrenching of the depository institutions industry from its sedate past was significantly accelerated. Bank and S&L executives who had long abided by the 9–3–3 rule—into the office at 9 in the morning, three hours for lunch, on the golf course by 3 in the afternoon—were finding themselves more and more challenged. Product and service decisions that had in years gone by been made by government decree were becoming the responsibility of private sector individuals. Some of them did not want the increased uncertainty. Others did not mind the uncertainty but, as events of the decade were to show, lacked the judgment and restraint to make wise choices on a consistent basis.

The Depository Institutions Deregulation and Monetary Control Act of 1980 contained other provisions in addition to those phasing out interest rate ceilings. One of the most intriguing, as least as much for its symbolic value as for its provable direct consequences, was the raising of the deposit insurance limit from $40,000 to $100,000.

Regarding direct consequences, probably the most notable was the impetus the action gave to the growth of brokered deposits. These are deposits that are gathered for or directed to banks or S&Ls by middlemen, or deposit-brokers. Brokered deposits became a big business in the 1980s, a business that had some detrimental results. A number of banks and S&Ls desirous of fast growth turned to brokered deposits to provide funds for their lending activities. The brokered deposits were often attracted by higher-than-average interest rates, a condition that the gradual elimination of the interest rate ceilings eventually made possible but that was jump-started by the raising of the deposit insurance limit. More than a few institutions that pursued the brokered deposits route to glory became casualties in the years ahead.

The connection between the raising of the insurance limit to $100,000 and the growth of brokered deposits lay principally in the fact that the interest rate ceilings did not apply to deposits of $100,000 or larger. The ceilings on deposits of $100,000 and above had been removed in 1970 to help stem the outflow of funds from large banks at the time of the Penn Central railroad crisis. Thus the raising of the insurance limit to $100,000 meant that the government guarantee of deposits had been expanded to a group of deposits not subject to interest rate ceilings. Almost immediately, entrepreneurs began bringing together packages of insurable deposits not subject to interest rate ceilings and institutions seeking funds.[6]

Also a factor, although a difficult one to quantify, in the connection between the raising of the insurance limit and the growth of brokered deposits was the handy nature of the $100,000 figure. A certificate of deposit of $100,000 had an easy marketability. Moreover, larger blocks of funds could be readily broken down into $100,000 blocks. Even the most mathematically impaired financial industry gnome could work with the nice round amount of $100,000.

But it is as a symbol, as evidence of a pervasive attitude, that the raising of the insurance limit is probably most instructive. The action was taken with very little debate and in part as a sop to those S&L industry executives who were opposed to the removal of interest rate ceilings. The nonanalytical manner in which the legal responsibility of the federal deposit insurance funds was more than doubled shows how cavalierly deposit insurance had come to be viewed. Forty years of practically no problems had lulled Congress, the regulators, and the industry into accepting deposit insurance as a free lunch. The benefits of deposit insurance seemed obvious, the principal one being a seemingly stable banking system. The costs, particularly a stagnating industry burdened with excess capacity and reluctant to change, were not so apparent.

Thus the bank and S&L industries entered the 1980s open to trouble. The world economic order had been changing. The volatility of economic life had long been on the increase. As a result of geographic and product limitations, the U.S. depository institutions industry was, in comparison to the industry in other nations, unconcentrated and segmented. Thousands of institutions existed in semiprotected geographic markets, enjoying only minimal competition from institutions with similar charters. The activities restrictions hindered innovation regarding products and services. Meanwhile, nondepository institutions not constrained by the pervasive geographical and product limitations were impinging more and more on the traditional businesses of banks and S&Ls. In short, the stability of the New Deal–era financial system was eroding, perceptibly in some ways, imperceptibly in others. Interest rate ceilings, a major support of the depository institutions industry, had become no longer tenable and had been ordered eliminated. The fun was about to begin.

THE 1980s

The economic and financial history of the 1980s defies easy characterization. For one thing, the decade abounded in contradictions. Amid widespread prosperity, sectors of the economy suffered significant downturns. Amid six-figure salaries on Wall Street for newly minted masters of business administration (MBAs), homelessness became a national issue. Amid a pervasive fear of inflation, financial strategies based on high and volatile interest rates produced enormous profits. Amid much concern about the detrimental effects of negative trade balances and federal budget deficits, gross domestic product enjoyed one of the longest continuous recorded rises in the nation's history. Amid cries of American economic stagnation, a period of almost unparalleled corporate restructuring took place.

Chronologically, the decade began with a slide into recession, which stretched 16 months from July 1981 to November 1982. Then followed the aforementioned lengthy, sustained economic expansion, an expansion so impressive that articles suggesting the demise of the business cycle began appearing. The business cycle, however, proved to be merely dormant, and the decade closed in a slide toward another recession, which arrived in July 1990 and lasted to March 1991.

Ideologically, the decade saw a resurgence of free market capitalism. Ronald Reagan was elected president in 1980 on a platform that in the domestic arena pledged to get the government off the peoples' collective back. Many of the economic and social programs descended from Franklin Roosevelt's New Deal and Lyndon Johnson's Great Society were perceived as unnecessary, indeed as hindrances to progress. The tax structure was viewed as onerous, a discourager of initiative and a zapper of the entrepreneurial spirit. The Reagan administration was remarkably successful in the degree to which it carried out its program. Under the rubric of "Deregulation," considerable reduction and simplification took place in many areas of federal regulation, including the banking area. And taxes were reduced, particularly for upper income taxpayers. As the decade proceeded, both deregulation and tax reduction were to have numerous and varied consequences, some foreseen, some unforeseen.

Morally, ethically, the decade certainly did not see a resurgence of much that was exemplary. Indeed, some would argue that the period was a nadir of sorts. Greed and ostentatious consumption were the order of the day for a sizeable segment of the population. Wall Street experienced a series of highly publicized insider trading scandals and securities laws violations. The tenor of the times was captured in Tom Wolfe's novel, *Bonfire of the Vanities*, in which the protagonist, a Wall Street trader, considers himself to be a "master of the universe." Main street was not immune to the stampede in search of wealth. In fact, a goodly proportion of the problems in the thrift and banking industries during the decade could be traced in the first instance to a certain moral laxity in the hinterlands. Bank and thrift directors and officers in a number of institutions were guilty of a variety of conflict of interest and self-dealing transgressions, some amounting to illegalities, some just unseemly. No better example of the prevailing attitudes can be found than that provided by the president, who was elected in 1992, and his spouse. The favoritism that they received in their real estate transactions and that she received in her commodities trading may not have amounted to violations of the law, but it did indicate a rather cavalier attitude regarding the ethics of associating public position with activities for private gain.

A central feature of the 1980s was debt. Between the mid–1950s and 1982, the ratio of domestic nonfinancial debt to nominal gross domestic product (GDP) had stayed within a relatively narrow band, averaging about 135 percent. In 1983, however, the ratio commenced a rapid rise, reaching almost 200 percent by the end of the decade.[7] Government, businesses, and households all participated in the debt binge. In the decade ending in 1992, federal government debt held by the public more than tripled, reaching $3.1 trillion. For the corporate sector, the debt-to-assets ratio reached a post–World War II record in 1990 of 32 percent.[8] The primary reasons for the increase in corporate sector debt were debt-financed acquisitions and stock repurchases. A term, "junk bonds," came into common usage to describe less-than-investment-grade debt instruments whose purpose was largely to finance corporate acquisitions and restructurings. For households, total debt of the household sector as a percentage of disposable personal income increased from 71 percent to 90 percent between 1980 and 1990.[9] Much of the increase was due to a rise in residential mortgages—during the period 1981–89, the ratio of mortgage debt to home values rose from 36 percent to 50 percent.[10]

The debt binge led to a general increase in the burden of servicing debts. For example, the ratio of interest cost to cash flow for nonfinancial corporations reached a post-World War II high of 25 percent in 1991.[11] The greater servicing burden contributed in turn to more downgradings of corporate debt, higher default rates on corporate bonds, and increases in business failures. It also depressed corporate profits. Whether measured relative to gross domestic product or corporate net worth, corporate profits in the 1980s were below the levels of the 1970s.[12] In the household sector, the ratio of debt service to disposable personal income rose from less than 15 percent in 1982 to over 19 percent in 1989.[13] Delinquency rates on mortgage loans and on consumer credit categories such as auto and credit card loans spiraled upward. Mortgage foreclosures rose steadily over the decade, and personal bankruptcies shot up after 1985.[14]

What caused the increase in debt? The tax deductibility of interest expense was certainly a factor. As inflation pulled interest rates higher in the 1970s and early 1980s, the fact that interest could be deducted in calculating taxes seemed actually to engender a sense of wealth on the part of some debtors. Theoreticians in finance gave respectability to the phenomenon by purporting to be able to calculate what a firm's optimum level of debt was. Debt has always been recognized as an ingredient of growth, but in the 1980s, debt's importance to growth came to be considered overriding. Indeed, individuals and businesses that shunned debt were looked upon with condescending pity.

The credit strains produced by the higher levels of debt and the greater debt servicing burdens found their way back to the providers of funds, including banks and S&Ls. The effects of debt were not the sole immediate cause of the difficulties depository institutions encountered in the 1980s, but they were certainly a major contributor to those difficulties.

NOTES

    1. *Economic Report of the President, February 1994* (Washington, D.C.: U.S. Government Printing Office, February 1994), Table B–62, p. 339.

    2. Ibid., Table B–72, p. 352.

    3. Board of Governors of the Federal Reserve System, *Guide to the Flow of Funds* Accounts (1993).

4.   The summary of the history of interest rate ceilings is based on Edward F. McKelvey, "Interest Rate Ceilings and Disintermediation," *Staff Economic Studies*, No. 99, Board of Governors of the Federal Reserve System (April, 1978).

5.   Constance Dunham, "The Growth of Money Market Funds," *New England Economic Review*, Federal Reserve Bank of Boston (September—October 1980), pp. 20–34.

6.   See Irving Sprague, "Unrelated Series of Events Led to S&L Crisis," *American Banker*, May 3, 1989, p. 4, for a description of events and consequences concerning interest rate ceilings and the raising of the deposit insurance limit.

7.   Board of Governors of the Federal Reserve System, *Flow of Funds*, p. 22 .

8.   Edward J. Frydl, "Overhangs and Hangovers: Coping with the Imbalances of the 1980s," *Annual Report 1991*, Federal Reserve Bank of New York, p. 16.

9.   Board of Governors of the Federal Reserve System, *Flow of Funds*.

10.   Frydl, p. 16.

11.   Ibid., p. 19.

12.   Ibid., p. 22.

13.   Ibid., p. 20.

14.   Ibid., p. 19.

3

A Crisis and a Shakeout: An Overview

As the 1970s gave way to the 1980s, the banking industry was ripe for change. Discerned by only a few, excess capacity provided the background. Interest rates—both the cost of the industry's major raw material and the price of its major products—were behaving in unaccustomed fashion. New aggressive competitors, aided and in some cases created by the computer-based revolution in communications and information processing, were appearing on the scene. Financial experimentation and risk-taking were coming to be held in high regard.

For the banking industry, the result of this volatile mix was a shakeout of sizeable proportions. Banks' partners in the depository institutions industry—savings and loan associations—were subject to the same structural and environmental factors. The impact on the S&L industry was more than a shakeout, however: it was a full-blown crisis. This chapter is an overview of the S&L crisis and banking troubles. Subsequent chapters examine the banking troubles, or shakeout, in greater detail.

The highlights of the S&L crisis and the banking troubles are as follows:

- Due to decades of geographic restraints, product limitations, and an overly protective deposit insurance system, the banking and S&L industries, and the financial industry of which they were a part, entered the 1980s burdened with excess capacity.
- The high and volatile interest rates in the late 1970s and early 1980s undermined the long-existing approach to profitability in savings and loans associations, which was: borrow for short terms at low rates, lend for longer terms at higher rates.
- In the 1970s and into the 1980s, both banks and S&Ls experienced increasing levels of competition from other sectors of the financial world. Because of the long-standing geographic and product restrictions, banks and S&Ls were constrained in their ability to respond.
- To aid the S&L industry, Congress and federal and state regulatory authorities in the early

1980s relaxed restrictions on activities. S&Ls' enthusiastic embrace of the new powers was not constrained by adequate supervisory oversight.

- The S&L industry suffered massive losses and eventually required a huge taxpayer bailout. The federal regulator and the federal insurer of S&Ls—the Federal Home Loan Bank Board (FHLBB) and the Federal Savings and Loan Insurance Corporation (FSLIC)—were legislated out of existence. The FHLBB was replaced by the Office of Thrift Supervision. The insurance function was given to the FDIC.
- As the S&L industry was experiencing its explosive expansion and implosive contraction, the banking industry and its regulators were hit by a rolling series of difficulties. Troubles in less-developed countries and in the energy, agriculture, and real estate sectors of the U.S. economy all had negative impacts on the health and profitability of banks.
- The real estate–related difficulties were the most widespread. The difficulties began in Texas and the Southwest and spread to the Northeast, the Southeast, and finally the West Coast.
- The banking industry's difficulties severely tested the FDIC and the bank deposit insurance system. Congress responded by significantly buttressing the bank supervisory system and by providing taxpayer backing for the Bank Insurance Fund.
- Largely in response to marketplace changes and until 1994 largely at the state level, interstate banking restrictions were relaxed. This relaxation contributed to a consolidation trend in which the numbers of bank and thrift organizations declined.
- Congress's efforts between 1980 and 1991 to deal with the turmoil in the depository institutions industry resulted in five major laws, each a reaction to the perceived difficulties of the moment and each pushing the regulation of depository institutions in significant new directions. The five laws were: the Depository Institutions Deregulation and Monetary Control Act of 1980 (DIDMCA); the Garn-St Germain Act of 1982; the Competitive Equality Banking Act of 1987 (CEBA); the Financial Institutions Reform, Recovery, and Enforcement Act of 1989 (FIRREA); and the Federal Deposit Insurance Corporation Improvement Act of 1991 (FDICIA).

The remainder of the chapter expands upon this summary. The S&L crisis is considered first. Then an overview of the banking troubles is presented.

THE THRIFT INDUSTRY

The crisis of the S&L industry in the 1980s was a two-step affair. The first step was relatively straightforward, its immediate cause relatively easy to pinpoint. That cause was high interest rates. The second step was significantly more complex and eventually much more severe. It concerned the sometimes contradictory responses of the industry, the industry's regulators, and Congress to those high interest rates and the various difficulties that ensued.

As institutions whose principal mode of operation was to fund long term loans with short term deposits, savings and loans were detrimentally affected by the prolonged period of high interest rates that occurred in the late 1970s and early 1980s. S&Ls sustained losses by having to pay higher rates on the short term deposits than they were earning on the long term loans. And the interest rate caps then in existence made keeping old deposits and acquiring new ones exceedingly difficult. In 1981, for example, the profits for the S&L industry were a negative $4.6 billion,[1] and FSLIC-insured institutions suffered net deposit withdrawals of $25.4 billion.[2]

Congress's initial answer to the problems created by the high interest rates was to provide for the phasing out of interest rate controls. As noted in the preceding chapter, this was done in the Depository Institutions Deregulation and Monetary Control Act of 1980. The relaxation and eventual elimination of the controls enabled both S&Ls and banks to stem the loss of deposits due to the inability to pay market rates of interest. Paying market rates of interest, however, only exacerbated the major difficulty facing a large proportion of S&Ls: supporting low-rate long term loans with high-rate short term liabilities.

Removal of interest rate ceilings was only the first of a number of steps Congress and the Federal Home Loan Bank Board—the federal regulator of S&Ls—took to aid the S&L industry in overcoming the interest rate–caused threat to its viability and in meeting other difficulties rising from changes in the financial marketplace. In total, the actions came to be referred to as the "deregulation" of the S&L industry. To generalize, the deregulatory steps beyond the removal of interest rate ceilings consisted of (1) the relaxation of capital and accounting standards and (2) the expansion of lending and investment powers.[3] Of great significance, the increased flexibility and freedom granted to S&Ls were not matched by increased supervisory efforts or resources. Indeed, a major cause of the subsequent troubles was inadequate supervision.

The relaxation of capital and accounting standards occurred in a variety of ways. One of the first major steps was the FHLBB's reduction in 1980 of the statutory reserve requirement—one of several measures of S&L capital—from 5 percent to 4 percent of insured deposits. The requirement was further reduced in 1982 to 3 percent. In 1981, the FHLBB authorized S&Ls to defer and amortize losses on the sale or other disposition of mortgage loans, mortgage-related securities, and debt securities. Previously, such losses had to be recognized immediately. Also in 1981, the FHLBB permitted troubled institutions to issue income capital certificates to bolster their capital positions. The certificates were purchased by the FSLIC with either cash or interest-bearing notes. In the Garn-St Germain Act of 1982, Congress appropriated the income capital certificate concept by authorizing a net worth certificate program for both banks and S&Ls. The program improved the financial appearance of banks and S&Ls with low net worth by permitting the institutions to count promissory notes from the appropriate federal regulator as capital. Among the FHLBB's actions in 1982 was an increase from 10 to 40 years in the period during which goodwill in merger transactions could be amortized. The effect was to significantly increase the reported, but not the real, income and capital of the S&L industry.

A retreat from the trend of standards relaxation began the following year, 1983, but several major capital-diluting steps still lay ahead. In 1985, the FSLIC began a Management Consignment Program to reorganize and recapitalize troubled institutions. The recapitalizations were largely paper transactions, being accomplished through the issuance of capital certificates. And in the Competitive Equality Banking Act of 1987, Congress instituted supervisory forbearance for "well-managed" under capitalized S&Ls.

Regarding the expansion of S&L lending and investment powers, the DIDMCA in 1980 was an important early step. Among its other deregulatory measures, that

act (1) removed a geographic limit on S&L lending; (2) allowed S&Ls to buy corporate debt and commercial paper up to 20 percent of assets and to invest up to 3
percent of assets in service corporations; and (3) expanded S&L authority to make
acquisition, development, and construction (ADC) loans. Meanwhile, several
states, notably California, Texas, and Florida, were aggressively broadening the
powers of state-chartered institutions. In 1980 and 1981, the FHLBB allowed
S&Ls to lend with loan-to-value ratios greater than 90 percent, to accept less than a
first lien on mortgage loans, and to hedge with financial futures. In addition, S&L
service corporation powers were expanded. In 1982, and on the liabilities side of
the ledger, the FHLBB removed restrictions on brokered deposits. Congress also
made significant liberalizing contributions in 1982, in the Garn-St Germain Act.
Prohibitions or limitations on nonresidential real estate lending, consumer lending,
commercial lending, and personal property leasing activities were relaxed.   These
many steps to expand the powers of S&Ls were not in themselves, and considered
individually, necessarily "bad." Indeed, in view of the changes taking place in the
financial marketplace, some of them may have been unavoidable, even desirable.
The liberalizing steps, however, were not accompanied by adequate oversight.
Many S&L executives reacted to the freer environment like small children turned
loose without parental oversight in the Halloween candy. The unrestrained gorging
was unsurprising, and the unpleasant consequences were not unforeseeable.

The resources and efforts of government supervisors were insufficient to halt a
rapid growth in imprudent lending and investing. Moreover, fraud and insider
abuse began surfacing with unsettling frequency. Attempts by supervisors to
handle troubled institutions with a minimum initial outlay of government funds
compounded the difficulties. Acquisitions of institutions were permitted in which
acquirers put little or no capital at risk. Unhindered by either government supervision or fear of losing their investments, more than a few such acquirers treated
their acquisitions as spigots on the pipelines of the nation's financial flows.

One further major ingredient interacted with the loosened capital and accounting
standards, expanded lending and investment powers, and inadequate supervision to
produce the S&L debacle of the latter half of the 1980s. That ingredient was an
exaggerated swing of the real estate cycle. Real estate markets expanded rapidly in
the early– and mid–1980s and contracted precipitously as the decade neared its
end. A portion of the expansion and contraction was undoubtedly the natural
workings of the marketplace. The pent-up demand that the high interest rates of the
early 1980s had produced led to overbuilding, which in turn caused retrenchment.
Just as important in the swing, however, were government actions and policies that
first encouraged and then discouraged flows of funds to real estate.

For some time, the semigovernment mortgage agencies—the Federal National
Mortgage Association, the Government National Mortgage Association, and the
Federal Home Loan Mortgage Corporation—had been bringing forth, in
conjunction with private sector participants in the capital markets, a variety of
innovative mortgage packaging techniques and products. The innovations widened
the circle of potential real estate investors.

Congress contributed to the upswing in the real estate cycle by tax cuts in 1981 and through the Secondary Mortgage Market Enhancement Act in 1984. The 1981 tax cuts contained accelerated depreciation provisions and investment tax credits that made real estate investments extremely attractive. The 1984 law reduced state barriers to investment in mortgage-related securities.

But then, as many real estate sectors were probably getting ready to cool of their own accord, Congress inadvertently accelerated the downturns with the Tax Reform Act of 1986. That law reduced depreciation benefits, restricted passive loss deductions, and eliminated favorable treatment for capital gains. The reduction in the attractiveness of real estate as an investment was both substantial and abrupt. Over the next few years, real estate values in many areas declined significantly. Commercial properties were particularly hard hit. S&Ls that had helped fuel the speculative binges of the early 1980s found themselves burdened with defaulting borrowers and falling collateral values. Although many of the post–1986 S&L failures were undoubtedly already foreordained, the Tax Reform Act of 1986, by suddenly altering the real estate investment climate, did the industry no favors.

By the middle of the decade, S&L executives were making extensive use of the increased powers they had been given by Congress, state legislatures, and the regulators. Between 1982 and 1985, industry assets grew 56 percent, from $686 billion to $1,070 billion.[4] The share of the nonresidential mortgage loan market controlled by S&Ls in 1980 was 11 percent. By 1985, the S&L proportion had risen to 30 percent.[5] Home mortgage loans—the traditional mainstay of S&Ls—fell from 67 percent of S&L assets in 1980 to 42 percent in 1985.[6] Newcomers rushed to the industry: 133 new S&L charters were issued in 1984, 173 the following year.[7]

Also by mid-decade, signs of the coming disaster were surfacing rapidly. In 1978, the mortgage delinquency rate for Federal Savings and Loan Insurance Corporation (FSLIC)-insured institutions had been under 1.5 percent. In 1986, it was 5 percent.[8] S&L industry profits for 1986 were an anemic $131 million. The previous year they had been $3.7 billion.[9] By one count, 46 FSLIC-insured institutions with assets totaling $12 billion failed in 1986.[10] At an estimated cost of $3.1 billion, these failures rendered the FSLIC fund insolvent.[11] In 1987, the S&L industry suffered a loss of $7.8 billion.[12] Forty-seven institutions with assets of $11 billion failed, at an estimated cost of $3.7 billion.[13]

Reaction to the developing crisis was increasing, but the taking of effective corrective steps was severely hindered by a number of factors. A general disbelief that the problems were really as bad as they seemed was widespread. The complexity and esoteric nature of the difficulties discouraged examination by the media. A politically powerful S&L industry lobby vehemently fought any reexamination of the liberalizing moves of the early 1980s and even the smallest attempt at increased supervision. Involvement of both political parties in industry problems—at the policy as well as individual levels—discouraged congressional and Executive Branch action, particularly during the 1986 and 1988 election years.

Congress's first effort to deal with the snowballing situation was tentative. The Competitive Equality Banking Act of 1987 authorized a $10.8 billion recapitalization of the FSLIC and called for supervisory forbearance for "well-managed" undercapitalized institutions. The act did little to staunch the hemorrhaging that was taking place in the S&L industry, and the $10.8 billion was quickly perceived as inadequate. In 1988, 205 S&Ls with assets of $100 billion failed. The estimated cost of the failures was $31.2 billion.[14] The FSLIC reported a deficit of $75 billion.[15]

Tentative was not how the next congressional effort could be characterized. Shortly after taking office in 1989, President George Bush sent a massive, complex S&L industry restructuring bill to Capitol Hill. The resulting legislation was the Financial Institutions Reform, Recovery, and Enforcement Act (FIRREA). The FHLBB and the FSLIC were abolished. S&L industry oversight was moved to a newly created agency in the Department of the Treasury, the Office of Thrift Supervision (OTS). The FSLIC's insurance functions were transferred to the FDIC. Responsibility for dealing with failed S&Ls was given to another newly created organization, the Resolution Trust Corporation (RTC), which was to accomplish its task and go out of existence at year-end 1996.[16]

A few of FIRREA's provisions—probably more than a few—went too far, thus compounding the difficulties. For example, S&Ls were required to dispose quickly of their junk bond inventories. In complying, some S&Ls sustained what might have been unnecessary losses, and the already weakened junk bond market may have received an additional unnecessary jolt.

Time, the exit from the industry of the worst performers, declining interest rates, and human effort eventually alleviated the S&L crisis, at a total estimated cost of $160 billion, excluding interest. From 1989 to June 30, 1995, when its authority to close failed thrifts expired, the RTC resolved 747 institutions with aggregated assets of $402 billion.[17] Most of the institutions were taken over in the first years of the RTC's existence.[18] What remained of the S&L industry—1,215 OTS-supervised institutions with assets of $777 billion at year-end 1997, down from 2,949 FSLIC-insured institutions with assets of $1,351 billion at year-end 1988—slowly returned to profitability. In 1988, the profitability nadir, the S&L industry lost $13.4 billion. The losses decreased in 1989 and 1990 to $6.2 billion and $2.9 billion, respectively. The industry finally posted a positive net income of $1.8 billion in 1991. The black ink continued in the years that followed. Industry net income for 1997 was $6.5 billion.[19]

Over a period of little more than a decade, the thrift industry first was severely threatened, then enjoyed enormous growth, then was virtually decimated, and finally emerged shrunken but profitable. Notwithstanding the recovery, the future of the industry as a separate, distinct industry is difficult to predict. The return to profitability has not stopped the slide in industry size. The number of thrifts has declined each year since the OTS's establishment in 1989. Aggregate assets declined initially, reaching $775 billion in 1993; at year-end 1997, assets were $777 billion. In the Deposit Insurance Funds Act of 1996, Congress mandated a merger of the deposit insurance funds for the bank and thrift industries—the Bank Insurance Fund and the Savings Association Insurance Fund—if no savings associations exist on the date specified for the merger, January 1, 1999. The assumption is that the savings association charter can be merged into the bank charter by that time. The thrift industry still has a fair amount of political power, however. In addition, the industry has a defender in a government agency, the OTS, that would go out of business if its constituency ceased to exist. Thus the legislated demise of the thrift industry appears to be no sure thing.

THE BANKING INDUSTRY

The difficulties that beset the banking industry in the 1980s and very early 1990s differed in several important respects from the problems of the S&L industry. First and foremost, the rise in interest rates in the late 1970s and early 1980s was much less a problem for banks—at least commercial banks—than it was for S&Ls. Although commercial banks were subject to the interest rate caps on deposits and consequently experienced some outflow of funds, they were not burdened with large proportions of long term fixed-rate assets. Commercial bank assets generally had much shorter maturities than did the mortgage loans of the S&Ls. Consequently, commercial banks could adjust upward the price of loans and other assets as the cost of funds—the rates paid on deposits—rose in response to market forces.

An exception to the generalization of the effects of interest rate rises on banks concerned a subset of the species—mutual savings banks. Like S&Ls, with which they shared the rubric "thrifts," mutual savings banks, found largely in the Northeast, were primarily in the business of real estate lending. As interest rates rose, their large inventories of fixed-rate mortgage loans declined in value, and they were unable to match increases in the cost of funds with increases in revenues. Their troubles, however, were not as broadly devastating as those of the S&L industry. For one thing, mutual savings banks constituted a relatively small proportion of the total banking industry. For another, the regulator of most savings banks, the FDIC, was much less indulgent than the S&L regulator, the FHLBB. Savings banks received a limited degree of temporary forbearance, but nothing comparable to the extent of the official kindness shown S&Ls. Problems were not compounded by a wholesale relaxation of accounting rules and product restrictions, and supervision was not curtailed.

Indeed, as a general matter, the supervisory system for banks was superior to the system for S&Ls. The primary federal S&L regulator, the FHLBB, was charged with being both a supervisor of S&Ls and a promoter of the home-financing industry. This dual focus probably increased the S&L supervisory system's susceptibility to the badgering and entreaties of what was at the time one of Washington's most powerful, and myopic, lobbies.

Another way in which banking industry problems differed from S&L industry problems was that the banking problems were for the most part regional in scope. Thus the entire industry was not hit by difficulties at once. The industry and its regulators were able to deal with troubles in more manageable portions than were the S&L industry and its regulators.

Four major sets of difficulties challenged the banking industry and its regulators in the 1980s and early 1990s. These four sets of difficulties concerned less-developed countries, agriculture, energy, and real estate lending, with the last being the most damaging. The four problem areas have a similarity. Bank involvement in each was characterized by an exuberance fueled in part by the enthusiasm of other banks—the bandwagon effect. The exuberance and enthusiasm clouded the reality that too much of a good thing is possible. After the initial burst of bank lending in each area, further funds were chasing fewer viable projects and were advanced with inadequate attention to changing macroeconomic conditions.

The less-developed country (LDC) debt crisis was the outcome of massive flows of funds to the LDCs in the 1970s. Fueled in large measure by the "petrodollars" that the oil-exporting countries placed in international banks following the oil price rises during the decade, the lending was based on increasingly tenuous assumptions about LDC growth. The LDCs simply could not make bona fide economic use of the financial largess coming their way. The lending resulted in large increases in LDC external debt.

Mexico's announcement in August 1982 that it would be unable to meet its debt payments to foreign creditors brought an abrupt end to unrestrained lending and an abrupt start to the LDC debt crisis. Within the U.S. banking industry, the largest banks were the ones with the greatest LDC exposure and consequently the most affected. As a percentage of equity capital and reserves, the nontrade exposure of the average U.S. money-center bank to LDCs was 227 percent in 1982.[20] The announcement by Mexico began a multiyear work-out effort involving banks, governments in both debtor and creditor countries, and international organizations during which much of the LDC debt was restructured. The crisis's impact on U.S. banks was slow to be acknowledged in financial statements. Eventually, however, the piper had to be paid. In 1987 and again in 1989, U.S. money-center banks added substantially to reserves to provide for LDC debt losses. The effect in 1987 was especially noticeable, the increase in reserves being largely responsible for a decline in the return on assets for the banking industry from 0.61 percent in 1986 to 0.09 percent in 1987.[21]

By the end of the decade, concern about LDC debt had largely abated. The external debt burden for a number of the LDCs had been eased through various forms of debt restructurings. Many countries were enjoying sustained periods of growth. As for banks, their exposure to LDC debt problems had been significantly reduced. For example, the ratio of LDC nontrade exposure to equity capital and reserves for the average U.S. money-center bank had fallen from 227 percent in 1982 to 91 percent in 1989.[22]

Regarding agricultural lending, difficulties had surfaced by 1984 and were to be a concern for the next several years. The difficulties had their immediate origins in the previous decade. Led by export growth and rising commodity prices, in the 1970s, the farming sector of the economy enjoyed one of its more expansive periods. The boom had a substantial effect on the price of farm land, causing it to rise significantly. Expecting the good times to continue, many farmers borrowed heavily to expand operations, using the inflating real estate values to support the increases in debt.

As booms are wont to do, however, the agriculture boom of the 1970s came to an end. The particular macroeconomic forces that had helped produce it—strong growth in demand in the industrial economies, a cheap dollar, high inflation, and low real interest rates—suffered reversals as the new decade began. The value of farmers' main asset, land, plunged.[23] Farmers who had used rising real estate values to finance operations were forced to rely on cash flow from operations. In many instances, the cash flow, which was reduced because of the general fall in demand, was not sufficient to enable debt service obligations to be met. In consequence, farm lenders experienced large loan losses, and many of them failed. Agricultural banks, defined as banks in which agricultural loans amount to 25 percent or more of total loans, accounted for 32 percent of bank failures in 1984 (25 of 79), 54 percent in 1985 (65 of 120), 41 percent in 1986 (57 of 138), 30 percent in 1987 (56 of 184), and 14 percent in 1988 (28 of 200).[24] Fortunately from the standpoint of the banking system and its regulators, most of the failed agricultural banks were relatively small. Thus considered in isolation, the problems in agricultural lending, though significant, were not system-threatening.

Energy lending difficulties, centered in the Southwest but reverberating nationwide, were to pose a more formidable challenge to banking and its overseers. As was the case with agriculture, the energy-related lending difficulties of the 1980s had their origins in boom conditions in the 1970s. The boom was due to the huge increase in energy prices. For example, the price of domestic crude oil rose more than 700 percent between 1973 and 1981, from $4.17 to $34.33 per barrel.[25] Assuming that the power of the OPEC to control world oil prices would continue, many forecasters envisioned a barrel's cost at $50 or more before too long.

Such projections colored the lending decisions at many Southwest banks and S&Ls. The oil-price outlook implied strong economic growth and in-migration for the region. Banking institutions responded by lending aggressively to businesses that stood to benefit from these trends, principally oil and gas producers, construction firms, and real estate developers. A sizeable oil-price hike in 1981, from $24 to $34 per barrel, appeared to confirm the prevailing outlook for ever-increasing energy prices.[26]

But 1981 was the oil-price apogee. Prices began falling in the latter half of the year and did not find a bottom until past mid-decade. The 1986 price per barrel was just under $15.[27] The prognosticators had failed to foresee the increase in supply from non-OPEC producers and the significant reduction in demand due to conservation measures. They had also failed to discern the fragility of OPEC's own production agreements. As oil prices began falling, OPEC members sought to maintain their revenues by ignoring production quotas and raising output. This further increased supply and accelerated the downward movement of prices.

Economic growth in the Southwest slowed, stopped, and turned negative. Real estate values collapsed, and lenders of all types began feeling the effects. From 1980 through 1989, 535 banks failed in Texas, Oklahoma, and Louisiana, a total that was 50 percent of all U.S. bank failures during the period.[28] Some of the failures were of agricultural banks, but the majority succumbed to energy-related difficulties. By the end of the decade, 9 of the 10 largest banking organizations in Texas had been recapitalized with FDIC or other outside assistance.[29] Factors that combined with the energy boom-bust to produce the Southwest banking debacle included inadequate portfolio diversification, poor underwriting standards, weak internal controls on lending decisions, infrequent supervisory examinations, and unrealistic real estate valuations.

The effects of the energy-related lending difficulties were not confined to the

Southwest. Indeed, the largest U.S. bank failure, that of Continental Illinois National Bank and Trust Company in 1984, with assets of $33.6 billion, can be traced to troubles in the Oil Patch. Continental had purchased hundreds of millions of dollars of energy loans from Penn Square Bank, N.A., Oklahoma City, which failed in 1982. The large losses on these loans started a sequence of events that culminated in May 1984 in a massive run on Continental. The immediate spark was withdrawals of several billion dollars in deposits by European and Japanese depositors. Quick action by the FDIC and the other bank regulators stanched the run. A permanent reorganization and recapitalization, involving significant monetary assistance by the FDIC, was accomplished later in the year.[30] Although the regulators' actions alleviated the immediate crisis, the appropriateness was questioned by a number of critics, a topic covered in the next chapter.

Energy-related lending and the difficulties it encountered also contributed to the most significant assault of the period on the banking industry's well-being—the collapse of a nationwide real estate boom. An important part of the Southwest's energy euphoria in the early years of the decade was a surge in construction and real estate development. That surge outlived the energy boom itself and spread to much of the rest of the nation. The surge continued long after economic indicators should have persuaded perceptive real estate lenders and investors that a degree of caution was in order. For example, the vacancy rate for office buildings in 31 major markets rose from 4.9 percent in 1980 to 13.5 percent in 1983 to 16.5 percent in 1985. Yet the funds continued to flow. By 1991, the vacancy rate was 18.8 percent.[31]

Banks and S&Ls were important providers of funds for the real estate boom. S&L involvement was discussed earlier in this chapter. For banks, real estate loans rose from 14.5 percent of their assets in 1980 to 24.5 percent a decade later.[32] And as was the case with S&L real estate activity, the composition of bank real estate lending shifted toward riskier endeavors. The safer home mortgage lending became relatively less important, displaced by more volatile construction and commercial real estate lending. Furthermore, the underwriting standards for construction and commercial real estate lending were relaxed. High loan-to-value ratios, no take-out commitments, and reduced recourse to corporate strength became common.

In hindsight, discerning what happened in the real estate boom-bust of the 1980s —as well as the boom-busts regarding LDC, agricultural, and energy lending—is relatively easy. Determining why it happened is more difficult and not susceptible to much in the way of quantifiable answers. The ultimate "why" raises issues of human psychology, specifically the mind-sets that produce economic booms and busts. Charles Kindleberger discussed the human propensity for economic folly in his classic *Manias, Panics, and Crashes: A History of Financial Crises*.[33] More recently, James Grant described the 1980s in his book, *Money of the Mind*, in terms that give rise to visions of credit run amuck.[34] Whatever the causes, the financial world of the 1980s saw a reduction in caution and an increase in risk-taking. Being part of the financial world, banks were infected by these attitudes. Banks were also influenced by the changing nature of their business. For example, many corporate customers found cheaper financing elsewhere, such as in the commercial paper market. As they lost customers and saw more competition in some of their traditional areas of activity, banks turned to other fields, such as the risky world of real estate development.

Bank troubles grew throughout the decade. Insured bank failures from 1934 through 1981 totaled 586, an average of 12 a year. On a decade basis, 358 banks failed from 1934 through 1940, 61 banks in the 1940s, 28 in the 1950s, 50 in the 1960s, and 79 in the 1970s. The 1980s started normally enough, with 10 banks failing in 1981. In 1982, however, the figure jumped to 42. From 1982 through 1992, 1,484 banks failed, an average of over 130 a year and more than two and a half times the number of failures in the previous 48 years.[35] In 1984, FDIC insurance assessments on banks were, for the first time since the agency's founding, less than insurance outlays.[36]

Still, the banking system, including the industry's deposit insurance fund, appeared to be in reasonably good shape through the end of the decade, particularly when compared to the S&L industry and its defunct insurance fund. Despite insurance assessments not keeping pace with insurance costs after 1984, the bank insurance fund continued to increase, reaching its then apogee, $18.3 billion, in 1987. The increases were due to interest on the fund's investments in U.S. Treasury securities. In 1988 the fund declined to $14.1 billion, and in 1989 to $13.2 billion, but attention at the time was focused on the thrift industry and its problems. The FDIC was still respected enough in Congress to be given responsibility for overseeing the organization and operation of the RTC, the S&L cleanup agency. That mandate came in FIRREA.[37]

Within a very short time, however, the possibility of an S&L-type disaster in the banking industry moved to center stage. The reason for the concern was increasing awareness of the enormity of the real estate problems. The Southwest's difficulties had been known for some time. But as the 1990s dawned, the abysmal state of New England real estate markets became apparent. And it soon became obvious that conditions in the Southeast and on the West Coast were also poor. Lenders, including banks, suffered heavy losses. The FDIC bank fund fell to $4.0 billion in 1990, and expectations of further massive declines rapidly became widespread.

Fears that the banking industry was going the way of the S&L industry quickly grew. Also attracting adherents was a belief that the performance of the bank regulatory agencies in controlling bank risk-taking had been inadequate. This belief was reflected in the Federal Deposit Insurance Corporation Improvement Act of 1991 (FDICIA). A general thrust of that law was to curtail supervisory discretion. One important way this was done was to require that certain corrective actions be taken as an institution's capital ratios decline. The act also, among other things, (1) provided a Treasury line of credit for the deposit insurance system, (2) mandated annual examinations for banks and savings associations, (3) established a least-cost standard to be followed by the FDIC in resolving failing institutions,[38] (4) required the adoption of a risk-based deposit insurance assessment system, and (5) restricted the activities of state banks.

For 1991, the FDIC reported a balance for the bank deposit insurance fund of a negative $7.0 billion, which included a large reserve mandated by the General Accounting Office for future failures. The negative result confirmed for a number of observers the severity of the situation. Predictions of continued troubles and further declines in the fund were heard throughout 1992 and even surfaced prominently as a issue in the presidential election campaign in the fall.

The low-point was 1991, however. Due in part to low interest rates, 1992 turned out to be a year of record profits for the industry. The number of bank failures—122—though large, was considerably less than what had been expected. The bank deposit insurance fund recovered to essentially a break-even position: a negative $100 million. The good news continued in the succeeding years and was still underway in 1998. Each year has seen the profitability record of the previous year broken. In 1994, the balance of the Bank Insurance Fund passed the prior peak of $18.3 billion, reached in 1987, and finished the year at $21.8 billion. At year-end 1997, the balance was $28.3 billion.

As the bank and S&L industries and individual institutions were on their roller-coaster rides during the 1980s and early 1990s, they were also on a consolidation path. From year-end 1983 to year-end 1992, the number of commercial banks fell more than 20 percent, from 14,469 to 11,462. At year-end 1997, the number of commercial banks was 9,143, a decline of 37 percent since 1983.[39] From year-end 1988 to year-end 1997, the number of thrifts declined 59 percent, from 2,949 FSLIC-insured institutions to 1,215 OTS-supervised institutions.[40] From year-end 1984 to year-end 1997, the number of independent banking organizations—bank holding companies plus unaffiliated banks and thrifts—declined 40 percent, from 14,888 to 8,967.[41] By the mid-1990s, the excess capacity that had burdened the industries at the beginning of the 1980s and that was a cause of the subsequent problems had been at least somewhat alleviated.

An important reason for the consolidation was the growth of interstate operations. In 1980, interstate bank and S&L organizations were largely prohibited by law. The various marketplace changes and crises, however, prompted efforts to overcome or reduce the legal hurdles. Many of these efforts were at the state level and consisted of measures permitting holding companies to acquire subsidiary depository institutions in more than one state. A number of the federally encouraged acquisitions of failed or failing banks and S&Ls involved interstate transactions. Indeed, without the existence of interstate acquirers, the bank and S&L cleanups might have been even more costly.

Overemphasizing the significance in U.S. financial history of the growth of interstate banking operations would be difficult. The move to reduce and remove state barriers marked a radical reversal of a two-century-old approach to supervising and regulating banking. For the future, the increased competition should help to control the tendency toward industry excess capacity that can be an undesirable by-product of government oversight and supervision. In addition, by making institutions less vulnerable to economic declines in a single state or region, interstate operations should enhance industry stability. In 1994, the federal government, with the passage of the Riegle-Neal Interstate Banking and Branching Efficiency Act, finally became a firm supporter of the interstate movement. The act authorized bank holding companies to acquire banks located in any state. Equally as important, it also authorized, beginning June 1, 1997, and unless a state affirmatively opted out of the provision's coverage before then, interstate branching through bank mergers across state borders. States can go further than the federal requirement by authorizing the establishment of new interstate branches.

The bank troubles and S&L crisis of the 1980s and early 1990s sorely tested the federal oversight system for depository institutions. The S&L crisis was the much more serious. The S&L industry was decimated, and the federal structure for regulating and supervising the industry was revamped. The banking troubles were milder. Both the banking industry and the federal banking agencies survived large-ly intact. But the survival has a downside. Some attribute banking's survival and remarkable recovery to the fundamental correctness of the regulatory system and to government actions to alleviate the troubles. The industry, however, might have survived not because of but in spite of the system and official actions. If this is the case, failure to grasp the true lessons of what transpired could raise the next banking crisis to the level of the 1980s' thrift debacle, resulting in a decimated industry and a disgraced regulatory structure.

NOTES

1. Office of Thrift Supervision, *Supervising Today's Thrift Industry* (December 1992), p. 1.

2. Federal Home Loan Bank Board, *Annual Report, 1986*, p. 6.

3. National Commission on Financial Reform, Recovery and Enforcement (NCFRRE), *Origins and Causes of the S&L Debacle: A Blueprint for Reform* (Washington, D.C., July 1993), contains a detailed description of the deregulatory steps taken by Congress and FHLBB regarding the S&L industry.

4. NCFRRE, p. 44.

5. Prudential-Bache Capital Funding, *Financial Strategies Group, A 1980s Retrospective of the Savings and Loan Crisis* (Prudential-Bache Capital Funding, 1990).

6. James R. Barth, *The Great Savings and Loan Debacle* (Washington, D.C.: The AEI Press, 1991), p. 25.

7. Prudential-Bache.

8. Ibid.

9. Barth, p. 25.

10. Ibid., p. 32.

11. Federal Home Loan Bank Board, *Annual Report, 1986*, p. 25.

12. Federal Home Loan Bank Board, *Annual Report, 1987*, p. 5.

13. Barth, p. 32.

14. Ibid.

15. Federal Home Loan Bank Board, *Annual Report, 1988*, p. 36.

16. The Resolution Trust Corporation Completion Act of 1993 changed the RTC's termination date from December 31, 1996, to December 31, 1995.

17. General Accounting Office, *Resolution Trust Corporation's 1995 and 1994 Financial Statements* (GAO/AIMD-96-123, July 1996).

18. The numbers of institutions taken over by the RTC by year were: 1989, 318; 1990, 213; 1991, 144; 1992, 59; 1993, 9; 1994, 2; and 1995, 2. Resolution Trust Corporation, *Statistical Abstract, August 1989/September 1995*, p. 9.

19. See Office of Thrift Supervision, *Savings & Home Financing Source Book, 1988*; *Supervising Today's Thrift Industry* (December 1992); *Quarterly Financial Results & Condition of the Thrift Industry, 4th Quarter, 1997*. See also, Jonathan L. Fiechter, *Testimony Concerning the Condition of the Thrift Industry Before the Committee on Banking, Housing, and Urban Affairs, U.S. Senate*, September 22, 1994. Net income for OTS-supervised institutions for 1992 to 1997 was: 1992, $5.1 billion; 1993, $4.9 billion; 1994, $4.3 billion; 1995, $5.4 billion; 1996, $4.8 billion; and 1997, $6.5 billion. But for a special assessment to

capitalize the Savings Association Insurance Fund, 1996 net income would have been an estimated record $6.9 billion.

20. Gary S. Fissel, "The Anatomy of the LDC Debt Crisis," *FDIC Banking Review* (Spring–Summer 1991, Vol. 4, No. 1) p. 10.

21. Calculated from Federal Deposit Insurance Corporation, *Historical Statistics on Bank-ing, 1934–1991*, Tables CB–7, CB–12.

22. Fissel.

23. See John Rosine and Nicholas Walraven, "Drought, Agriculture, and the Economy," *Federal Reserve Bulletin* (January 1989), p. 7.

24. Total bank failures for each year are from FDIC *Annual Report, 1991*, Table A, p. 127. Agricultural bank failures are from the following FDIC *Annual Reports*: 1986, p. 8; 1987, p. xvi; 1988, p. xvi.

25. John O'Keefe, "The Texas Banking Crisis: Causes and Consequences, 1980–1989," *FDIC Banking Review* (Winter 1990, Vol. 3, No. 2), Table 5, p. 17.

26. Ibid. The price is the domestic crude oil refiner acquisition cost.

27. Ibid.

28. Gregory K. Gibbs, "Distribution of Failed Banks by State and by Type of Transaction," Unpublished paper prepared in the Banking Statistics Section, Division of Research & Statistics, Federal Deposit Insurance Corporation, March 16, 1990.

29. O'Keefe, p. 1.

30. See Federal Deposit Insurance Corporation, *Annual Report, 1984*.

31. CB Commercial/Toro Wheaton Research. Vacancy rates are reprinted in various issues of *The Real Estate Report*, Division of Research and Statistics, Federal Deposit Insurance Corporation.

32. Calculated from Federal Deposit Insurance Corporation, *Historical Statistics on Banking, 1934–1991*, Tables CB–12 and CB–14.

33. Charles P. Kindleberger, *Manias, Panics, and Crashes: A History of Financial Crises* (New York: Basic Books, 1978).

34. James Grant, *Money of the Mind* (New York: Farrar Straus Giroux, 1992).

35. Federal Deposit Insurance Corporation, *Annual Reports*.

36. Ibid. Data in the subsequent paragraphs on bank failures and on balances of the deposit insurance fund are also from the FDIC's *Annual Reports*.

37. The FDIC's oversight of the RTC was removed by the Federal Deposit Insurance Corporation Improvement Act of 1991.

38. Section 141 of FDICIA, 12 U.S.C. §1823(c)(4), requires the FDIC to use the "least costly" method of resolving failed or failing banks. A systemic risk exception exists for large institutions. The least-cost standard replaced the cost test that the FDIC had been using since 1951 and that had been codified in the 1982 Garn-St Germain Act. Under the cost test, financial assistance provided by the FDIC to aid in the acquisition of a troubled bank by another institution could not exceed the cost of liquidating the bank and paying off only its insured deposits.

39. FDIC, *Annual Reports*, individual years; *Historical Statistics on Banking, 1934–1992*; *Statistics on Banking*, individual years.

40. Office of Thrift Supervision, *Savings & Home Financing Source Book, 1988*; *Quarterly Financial Results & Condition of the Thrift Industry* (4th Quarter, 1996).

41. FDIC, *Quarterly Banking Profile; Graph Book* (4th quarter, 1997).

4

Too Big To Fail:
Sound Bite in Search of a Policy

When Chairman Bill Isaac left the FDIC in 1985, he departed with the admiration and respect of the agency's staff. Within a few years, however, more than a few members of that staff regarded Mr. Isaac as the Benedict Arnold of bank regulation. His sin? He publicly questioned the FDIC's actions concerning the largest bank failure in U.S. history, actions that he himself helped shape, and that he oversaw and approved.[1] One cannot fully appreciate the enormity of Mr. Isaac's sin unless one remembers that questioning its own past is not one of a bureaucracy's strong points, and the FDIC is nothing if not a bureaucracy.

The bank in question was Continental Illinois National Bank and Trust Company. It was the biggest victim of the energy lending spree of the early 1980s. It was rescued by the federal banking regulators, with the FDIC playing a crucial role. The rescue precipitated a debate on the handling of bank failures that lasted for the rest of the decade. Moreover, at its heart the debate was about much more than bank failures. It was about the structure of banking in the United States and was a continuation of the small bank-big bank arguments that had been ongoing since the nation's founding. It encompassed elements of states' rights and populism. In the years following the Continental rescue, this two-centuries old debate became focused on the concept of "too big to fail."

CONTINENTAL ILLINOIS

The rescue of Continental Illinois National Bank and Trust Company (NB&TC) in 1984 was, and remains to this day, the largest bank resolution in U.S. history. The bank's parent holding company was Continental Illinois Corporation. The size of the transaction attracted considerable public attention, which contributed to issues concerning bank resolutions receiving a degree of public scrutiny not previously experienced. One particular issue was whether large banking organizations in trouble received preferential treatment from government regulators.

At year-end 1983, less than six months before its troubles surfaced, Continental Illinois NB&TC, with assets of $33 billion, was the seventh largest bank in the United States. The holding company was the eighth largest holding company. The immediate cause of Continental's troubles was a traditional bank run with a high-tech cachet: rather than physically lining up at the doors, withdrawing depositors made their attack through electronic transfers. The longer term causes of the difficulties involved declines in lending standards and too great an emphasis on growth.

Continental had grown rapidly in the late 1970s. Between 1976 and 1982, its loan portfolio increased almost 200 percent, from $11.6 billion to $34 billion. For the same period, the assets of the U.S. banking industry as a whole increased just 80 percent. Energy lending was a significant contributor to Continental's growth. In particular, by 1982 the Chicago-based institution held approximately $1 billion in oil and gas loans originated by Penn Square Bank, N.A., of Oklahoma.[2] Penn Square, with assets of approximately $500 million, considerably less than the total assets it had originated but sold to others such as Continental, failed in July of 1982, a victim of lending practices that were little more than speculation. Its resolution was handled by closing the bank and paying off insured depositors to the extent of their insured deposits. It was the largest bank payoff, a subcategory of bank resolution methods, in the history of the FDIC. The Penn Square failure was the flame that lit the fuse of Continental's implosion.

Awareness of the relationship between Continental and Penn Square caused the investing community deep concern. Continental Illinois Corporation's stock dropped from $25 a share in June 1982 to $16 a share in mid-August. The stock recovered before the end of the year and reached $26 in the first quarter of 1983, but earnings for 1982 were only a third of what they had been in 1981. Exacerbating Continental's difficulties were its loan exposures in a number of bankruptcies in 1982 and in the international debt crisis that burst on the scene in August of the year when Mexico announced it would be unable to meet debt payments to foreign creditors.

Continental's earnings for 1983 were an improvement over 1982, but much of the improvement was attributable to asset sales and extraordinary items rather than to continuing operations. Domestic funding sources became more difficult to tap, and Continental turned increasingly to the Eurodollar market, which was more expensive.

Exactly what set off the run on Continental in May of 1994 was never isolated. The sale of a profitable credit card operation in March, anemic first quarter earnings, an allusion to troubles by television commentator Robert Novak, and a perhaps overly emphatic denial of difficulties by Continental itself have all been cited.[3] What is clear is that the run occurred. In the ten days preceding the announcement of FDIC assistance on May 17, over $6 billion was withdrawn from Continental, practically all of it through wire transfers. In the assistance package announced on May 17—a package worked out by the FDIC, the Federal Reserve

System, the Comptroller of the Currency, and private bankers—the FDIC made a $2 billion subordinated loan to Continental. The bankers participated in $500 million of the loan. In the announcement following the loan, the FDIC, the Federal Reserve, and the OCC stated that the assistance was temporary and designed to ensure the bank's liquidity until a permanent resolution could be arranged. The temporary package also included assurances that the bank would have access to the Federal Reserve System to meet any extraordinary liquidity requirements.

In late July 1984, after more than two months of exhaustive efforts by, and some degree of acrimony among, the federal banking regulators and the Department of the Treasury, a plan for a permanent resolution of Continental's difficulties was agreed upon. The FDIC took $4.5 billion in bad loans from Continental. The FDIC paid for the loans by assuming $3.5 billion in loans to Continental from the Federal Reserve Bank of Chicago. The result of this portion of the transaction was that Continental immediately wrote off a $1 billion loss. The loss was replaced by the injection by the FDIC of $1 billion into the parent holding company. In return, the FDIC received preferred stock in the holding company. The $1 billion was down streamed by the holding company into the bank in the form of equity capital.

Among the issues the banking regulators and the Department of the Treasury grappled with regarding the resolution of Continental Illinois was the threshold one of deposit payoff versus continued existence. Why not simply close the bank and pay off the insured deposits?

From almost the beginning of its existence in 1933, the FDIC has had two basic options regarding a failed or failing bank: (1) close the bank permanently and pay off the insured deposits[4] or (2) keep the bank itself or its remnants in existence. The second alternative is most often accomplished by having another bank acquire the failed or failing bank.[5] Since 1950, however, the FDIC has had the power to keep a failing bank in existence by infusing funds directly, as was done in the Continental case.[6]

Until the 1990s, a crucial distinction between closing a bank and paying off depositors, on one hand, and keeping the bank or its remnants in existence—either through an acquisition or by a direct infusion of FDIC funds—on the other, was that only with the first method did uninsured depositors suffer losses. Any of the variants in the second category practically always resulted in all depositors—insured and uninsured—receiving full protection, although a point often overlooked was that management and shareholders were not protected: top management was usually replaced and shareholders usually suffered losses.

Today, as a result of Section 141 of the Federal Deposit Insurance Corporation Improvement Act of 1991, the FDIC is required to use the "least costly" method of resolving failed or failing banks.[7] In implementing the provision, the FDIC developed a new method for merging a failed or failing bank into a healthy one. Under the new method, only the insured deposits of a failed or failing bank are assumed by the acquiring institution. Uninsured deposits are not assumed or otherwise protected. The FDIC calls these transactions "purchase and assumption-insured deposits only" transactions. In 1992, the year after FDICIA's enactment and even before Section 141 went into effect, they accounted for 42, or 34 percent, of the

122 failed or failing bank cases resolved by the FDIC.

The FDIC did make one attempt prior to FDICIA to reduce the protection afforded uninsured depositors. In 1983–84, the agency, under Chairman Isaac, experimented with a "modified payout" procedure. Under this procedure, the FDIC advanced to uninsured depositors and other creditors an amount based on the anticipated recoveries of the failed bank's assets. Normally, liquidation recoveries were paid out to uninsured depositors and creditors only when received. The ultimate intent of the modified payout experiment was to increase market discipline by placing uninsured depositors and creditors at a greater risk of loss. More apprehension on the part of depositors and creditors supposedly would result in more marketplace restraints on management. If the modified payout procedure had proved successful, the acquisition method of handling failed banks—in which uninsured depositors and other creditors were invariably fully protected—would have given way in many instances to liquidations and the accompanying payoffs of insured depositors only. The immediate partial payments provided under the modified payoff procedure were apparently viewed as making the shift from acquisitions to deposit payoffs more palatable. The modified payoff experiment, however, fell victim to the Continental crisis, although in hindsight the aban-donment of the experiment does not appear to have been absolutely necessary. Perhaps the controversy surrounding the Continental crisis temporarily curtailed the FDIC's appetite for experimentation. In addition, at least some in the agency apparently did not view the concept of increased depositor discipline as practical.[8]

In any case, the modified payout experience of 1983-84 was an aberration for the pre–FDICIA period. Prior to FDICIA, two distinct alternatives existed for handling a failed or failing bank: (1) closing the bank and paying off insured deposits or (2) keeping the bank in existence through an acquisition or the provision of assistance. Uninsured depositors and other creditors suffered under the first alternative, not so under the variants of the second.

One of the considerations in the choice between the two alternatives, and one only occasionally acknowledged explicitly, was ease of administration.[9] The larger the bank, the more administratively and logistically difficult it was to close the doors, pay off the depositors, and liquidate the assets. This ease-of-administration consideration could combine with concerns about the effect on a community of shutting down a large institution, and with other factors, such as a perceived higher franchise value for larger institutions, to create a correlation between the size of a troubled institution and the way that regulators preferred to handle it. The larger the bank, the greater the subtle pressure bank regulators felt to find an alternative to closing the doors and paying off depositors.

And indeed an actual correlation between bank size and resolution method did exist, although the relationship was not as clear-cut as many discussants of the issue would have one believe. For example, for banks that failed during the period 1986–1992, the average assets of the 224 institutions that were liquidated, with only the insured deposits fully paid off, was $60 million.[10] This was considerably below the average assets of $207 million for the 928 institutions that were resolved through some form of acquisition or open bank assistance, both of which resulted in uninsured deposits being fully protected. For two of the years, however, the average assets of the liquidated and uninsured-deposits-unprotected banks exceeded the average assets of the uninsured-deposits-protected banks. In 1987, the average assets of the 51 uninsured-unprotected resolutions was $48 million, while the average assets of the 152 uninsured-protected resolutions was $45 million. And in 1990, the average assets of the 20 uninsured-unprotected resolutions was $125 million, while the average assets of the 149 uninsured-protected resolutions was $89 million.

But as a generalization, the statement was accurate that troubled large banks were more likely than troubled small banks to be handled in a manner resulting in full protection for uninsured depositors. This being the case, the potential existed for the development of a perception of unequal treatment between depositors and other creditors of troubled large banks and those of troubled small banks. Prior to 1984, the perception was largely uncrystallized, due most likely to the small number of bank failures and their generally unspectacular nature. Uneasiness existed about the differing effects on uninsured depositors of the liquidation-and-payoff alternative versus the keep-the-bank-or-its-remnants-in-existence alternative, but the debate focused as much on the supposed lack of depositor or marketplace discipline as on bank size.[11]

Continental Illinois, however, changed the focus of the debate, and considerably broadened the interested audience. The ingredient added by Continental Illinois was a factor that had been present in only one or two troubled bank cases over the preceding half-century. That ingredient was the stability of the banking system itself.

As the seventh largest bank in the nation, Continental was difficult for the banking regulators to view in isolation. It had a large correspondent business.[12] Almost 2,300 small banks had a total of nearly $6 billion at risk in the Chicago institution. The exposures of 66 of them were greater than their capital, and the exposures of another 113 were in excess of 50 percent of their capital. If Continental were closed and only insured deposits made whole—insured deposits amounted to little more than $3 billion of Continental's more than $33 billion in liabilities—at least some of these U.S. banking customers would have their own existences threatened. In addition, the international banking community was closely watching the actions of the U.S. banking regulators. Losses by uninsured depositors would have significantly reduced foreign faith in the U.S. banking system. The consequences of such a loss of trust on the part of foreign depositors and investors were, of course, unknowable beforehand but not pleasant for those responsible for the health of the U.S. banking system to contemplate.

Thus the alternative of closing Continental and paying off only insured depositors was not an attractive option for U.S. banking regulators. In their view, the potential impact of this alternative on the stability of the U.S. banking system made preserving Continental as an ongoing institution, either by arranging an assisted acquisition or by propping up Continental itself, an imperative. An appropriate acquirer could not be found, so the FDIC resorted to its authority to prop up an existing institution.

In the public and private sector analyses that followed the Continental rescue, the relationships among bank size, the stability of the banking system, and resolution methods received considerable attention. A simplistic phrase—too big to fail—soon gained popularity as a way of quickly referring to the relationships and the issues they raised. Those issues included not only procedural matters: What was the threshold at which a bank supposedly became too big to fail? Who should make the determination? Was including a bank's parent holding company in a resolution permissible? They also encompassed equity, fairness, and other concerns: Could the perceived difference in treatment between depositors and creditors at large banks and those at small banks be somehow eliminated or mitigated? If some banks were too big to fail, how could the benefits of depositor and market discipline be resurrected?

"Too big to fail" became more than a simplistic way to refer to a number of related complex and difficult issues, however. In an age of policy by sound bites, "too big to fail," or TBTF as it was quickly acronymed, was just too catchy to fail. It was one of those phrases that takes on a life of its own. It became, in the minds of many, an official "policy" of the U. S. government and was both attacked and defended on the basis of that supposed status.

THE DEBATE

Irvine Sprague, an FDIC director at the time of the Continental rescue, related in *Bailout*, a memoir of his participation in bank rescue efforts of the 1970s and early 1980s,[13] his initial encounter with the vehement visceral negative reaction on the part of a portion of the banking community. The encounter occurred just after the regulators acted in May 1984 to temporarily staunch the hemorrhaging at the bank. Mr. Sprague went to California to attend a meeting of the California Bankers Association. With pride and perhaps a bit too much self-satisfaction, he related the details of the events of the past few days. Upon finishing, he asked for questions, apparently expecting at the most a few mild inquiries.

What he got was a chorus of wrath and indignation. The Californians contrasted the Continental rescue in which uninsured depositors and creditors were protected from losses with the failure two weeks earlier of a bank five miles down the road. The $76 million National Bank of Carmel had been closed by its regulators, and only insured deposits had been made whole. Uninsured depositors and creditors of the failed bank were facing as yet undetermined losses, and loan customers were having to deal with the uncertainty attendant upon the disappearance of their lender.

The Californians' outcry presaged almost a decade of hand-wringing about and criticism of the treatment of troubled big banks. Often, the point of the anguish was difficult to determine, seemingly even for many of the anguishers themselves. Some critics genuinely believed that Continental should have been allowed to fail, and moreover that no bank was "too big to fail." These critics usually were fairly clear in their criticism. A larger group, however, simply were not happy with the fact that smaller banks in trouble were more likely to be closed than were larger banks in trouble. Some members of this group were even willing to acknowledge the reality that considerations about the overall stability of the economy might lead to disparate treatment between small and large banks. They just didn't like it. The more Machiavellian used the supposed advantage that large banks enjoyed as a result of being "too big to fail" to argue against attempts to remove or reduce the geographic and product restraints on the banking industry. If large banks had a competitive advantage as a result of being "too big to fail," smaller institutions and other industries should have offsetting competitive advantages in the form of protected franchises. Thus too big to fail was used to perpetuate the maintenance of the barriers that had created excess capacity in the financial industry.

Congressional hearings in the fall of 1984 set the tone of the discussion for the rest of the decade. C. Todd Conover, the Comptroller of the Currency, was grilled on September 19, 1984, before a subcommittee of the House Banking Committee. About midway through his lengthy interrogation, the following exchange took place:[14]

Chairman Fernand J. ST GERMAIN: Mr. Conover, where does Continental Illinois's rank in size among the banks of the United States of America? Is it 11th, 10th, 9th, 8th?

Mr. CONOVER: It seems to be moving [Author's note: sarcasm before Congress is not normally a wise practice].

Chairman ST GERMAIN: Where was it?

Mr. CONOVER: It was eighth, approximately.

Chairman ST GERMAIN: Number eight?

Mr. CONOVER: Yes.

Representative Chalmers P. WYLIE: You have 11 multinationals?

Mr. CONOVER: Right.

Chairman ST GERMAIN: All right. Ever see the fellow who is painting himself into that corner? He doesn't realize there is no door back there. And there is less floor for him to walk over. I got news for you. You are painting yourself in a corner because my question now is: Can you foresee, in view of all the reverberations internationally that you described, had Continental Illinois been allowed to fail, and all those people put out of work and all those corporations out of money and all those other banks that would have failed, in view of that, can you ever foresee one of the 11 multinational money center banks failing? Can we ever afford to let any one of them fail?

Mr. CONOVER: The answer to that, Mr. Chairman, is that we have got to find a way to. In order—

Chairman ST GERMAIN: You are not answering.

Mr. CONOVER: In order to have a viable system.

Chairman ST GERMAIN: Mr. Conover, you said you don't have in your hip pocket the solution for the small banks, and you are never going to have it. The fact of the matter is, as a practical matter, neither you nor your successors are ever going to let a big bank the size of Continental Illinois fail.

Mr. CONOVER: Mr. Chairman, it isn't whether the bank fails or not. It is how it is handled subsequent to its failure that matters. And we have to find a way. I admit that we don't have a way right now. And so, since we don't have a way, your premise appears to be correct at the moment.

Precisely what point Chairman St Germain, who incidentally after 28 years in

Congress was defeated in 1988 following revelations that he had been the recipient of much largess from lobbyists for the thrift industry, was trying to make is uncertain. He and his colleagues appeared to be engaged in an elaborate game of "Gotcha." But they seemed to have elicited no more than the obvious from Mr. Conover: large banks in difficulty posed troublesome problems for those government officials responsible for their handling. A political cynic might say that the browbeating of Mr. Conover was less about the pros and cons of rescuing Continental Illinois than about the upcoming 1984 presidential and congressional elections. After all, the House of Representatives was controlled by the Democrats, Chairman St Germain was a Democratic stalwart of the first order, and Mr. Conover was part of a Republican administration. The author, however, still has a high school civics view of government and is reluctant to believe that members of Congress would conduct hearings merely to score political points.

In any case, some commentators found more in Mr. Conover's words than a simple acknowledgment of the problems presented by large banks in difficulty. From his reluctant admission that the then-existing ways of dealing with large bank difficulties were not the best, a government "policy" of avoiding large bank failures emerged. Under the headline "U.S. Won't Let 11 Biggest Banks in Nation Fail," a *Wall Street Journal* journalist reported the day after the hearing:

Mr. Conover's statement was met by jibes from committee members, who said the government had created a new category of bank: the "TBTF" bank, for Too big to fail. Many banking observers had said that the Continental rescue in July indicated that regulators already had adopted such a policy, but Mr. Conover's testimony yesterday has the first time a government official acknowledged that such a policy existed.[15]

Almost 10 years later, the caveated words so painfully extracted from Mr. Conover were still being endowed with a certitude difficult to find in the transcript of the hearing. Writing in 1992, two members of the academic world stated:

In the wake of the Continental Illinois bank liquidity crisis, the Comptroller of the Currency testified to Congress on September 19, 1984, that some banks were just "too big to fail" (TBTF), and in these cases total deposit insurance protection would be provided, rather than enforcing the statutory $100,000 per account limit. In his testimony, the Comptroller admitted that banks included in the TBTF *policy* were the eleven largest. [Emphasis added.][16]

Later in their article, after a review of the history of the FDIC and its actions regarding troubles in large banks, the authors stated: "In September 1984, the Comptroller of the Currency formally announced the TBTF policy."[17]

Except for an accident of timing and perhaps a bit more success in resisting Congressional browbeating, the FDIC's Mr. Isaac could have joined Mr. Conover in the eyes of the banking world as a coauthor of the too-big-to-fail "policy." The accident of timing was that Mr. Isaac followed Mr. Conover at the witness table by more than two weeks. Mr. Conover testified on September 19. By the time Mr. Isaac testified on October 4, Mr. Conover had already become inextricably associated with too big to fail. Moreover, Mr. Isaac had the benefit of being forewarned about the path toward which he would be manhandled. Still, standing firm in the face of the congressional onslaught was no easy thing, as illustrated by the following exchange:

Mr. Bill PATMAN: Well, Mr. Chairman, if I may state my question at this point, you made a judgment that Continental was too big to fail.
Mr. ISAAC: No.
Mr. PATMAN: Isn't that true?
Mr. ISAAC: No; I made the judgment—
Mr. PATMAN: Too big a bank to fail?
Mr. ISAAC: I made the judgment that it would be cost effective, No. 1, to handle Continental the way we did, and, number—
Mr. PATMAN: That was irrelevant, though, that was irrelevant because you first—
Mr. ISAAC: It wasn't irrelevant to me.
Mr. PATMAN: You determined it was essential. It was not essential to your decision.
Mr. ISAAC: Cost was not the legal test we relied on, but that very much was the factor in my behavior. Now, I made, No. 1, a judgment that it was cost effective to handle Continental the way we did and, No. 2, that the consequences of handling it some other way would have been more severe than I cared to take responsibility for.
Mr. PATMAN: Let's take that viewpoint of it. Why don't you just say the impact of the failure of so large a bank was too great and that met the test of essentiality as far as you were concerned?
Mr. ISAAC: What I will say is the impact of paying off insured deposit accounts in Continental at that time could have been catastrophic.
Mr. PATMAN: And you would say the same thing about any other large bank?
Mr. ISAAC: No; I did not say that. I will not say that.
Mr. PATMAN: But if faced with the stark reality of another bank failing with the same impact as the failure of Continental would have had or resulted in, you would do the same thing, isn't that true, and reach the same conclusion?
Mr. ISAAC: I am not going to speculate on that. I was dealing with a specific problem—
Mr. PATMAN: It would be unfair to—
Mr. ISAAC: At a specific time.
Mr. PATMAN: If you run into another bank whose impact failure, the impact of which would be—
Mr. ISAAC: If you are telling me that if—
Mr. PATMAN: Excuse me—
Mr. ISAAC: If I get an identical set of circumstances, will I act in the same way? Yes, I will.   That is true.
Mr. PATMAN: If you get another bank about to fail that will cause the same impact that the Continental failure would have caused, you would do the same thing?
Mr. ISAAC: Depending on what other options I had at the time.
Mr. PATMAN: If you had the same options?
Mr. ISAAC: That is an identical situation. If you have an identical situation, I would act the same way because I am satisfied with what we did.

Thus Mr. Isaac managed, if just barely, to avoid an implication that there was a "policy" about too big to fail. The next day's news report in *The Wall Street*

Journal did not find in his testimony the formal government stance that the paper had discerned in Mr. Conover's testimony.[18] But the damage was done. The phrase was simply too cute for journalists, commentators, members and staff of Congress, and other assorted kibitzers to let die. The phrase took on a life of its own and in the minds of many was itself conclusive evidence of a government "policy."

As time passed, even some of the banking regulators fell into the "policy" trap. For example, in testimony before the Senate Banking Committee in July 1990, FDIC Chairman L. William Seidman stated unequivocally, that "the FDIC does not in fact have a Too Big To Fail policy." Yet several paragraphs later, in the same section of his testimony, he said: "Past experience in all major countries supports the contention that a Too Big To Fail policy exists, de facto if not de jure."[19]

Mr. Seidman was more circumspect in an appearance before a House subcommittee the following May. Perhaps his caution was a reaction to the ex-uberance with which both the subcommittee members and a Treasury Department official, Under Secretary Robert R. Glauber, assumed the existence of, and criticized, a too big to fail "policy." The occasion was one in a series of congressional hearings in 1991 as problems in the banking industry mounted. This particular hearing was on the "Economic Implications of the 'Too Big To Fail' Policy."[20] Appearing on a panel with Mr. Seidman and Mr. Glauber were Comptroller of the Currency Robert L. Clarke and Federal Reserve Board Governor John LaWare.

While the three regulators very carefully avoided using the phrase "too big to fail" and the word "policy" in proximity, neither the congressmen nor Mr. Glauber were so constrained. In his opening statement, Subcommittee Chairman Thomas R. Carper (D-Delaware) said that the purpose of the hearing was "to discuss the economic implications of the too-big-to-fail policy and proposed legislative changes to this policy."[21] Mr. Glauber was as equally blunt: "It is a pleasure to explain the administration's proposal to roll back the Federal Deposit Insurance Corporation's too-big-to-fail policy."[22]

When contrasted with statements of Mr. Seidman, Mr. Glauber's testimony is also instructive regarding a major confusion surrounding the so-called "policy." Mr. Glauber described the "policy" as resulting "in the protection of all uninsured deposits in most bank failures, particularly larger ones."[23] But according to Mr. Seidman, the FDIC had only invoked the too big to fail "doctrine"—he did not use the word "policy"—four times over the previous five years.[24]

Mr. Glauber was obviously viewing all failed or failing banks that were not actually liquidated but kept in existence through one means or another as being beneficiaries of a too big to fail policy. Mr. Seidman, on the other hand, apparently was equating too big to fail with the doctrine of essentiality. When it codified the cost test in the Garn-St Germain Act of 1982, Congress had provided an essentiality exception. If the FDIC determined the continued operation of a bank was essential to provide adequate banking services to the community, the deposit insurer did not have to find that a resolution method other than liquidation was less costly than liquidation in order to use the other method. The four cases over the previous five years in which the FDIC had resorted to the essentiality exception were Mr. Seidman's four invocations of the too big to fail doctrine.[25] No Congressman or other participant in the hearing called attention to the markedly different usages of the term which was the subject of the gathering.

The extent of the failure of Mr. Isaac, Mr. Seidman, and a few other regulators to prevent the spread of the belief that a too big to fail policy existed was revealed with the FDIC prepared its *History of the Eighties*. In the summary chapter, the very agency once headed by Messrs. Isaac and Seidman said: "At various times and for various reasons, regulators generally concluded that good public policy required that big banks in trouble be shielded from the full impact of market forces and that their uninsured depositors be protected. This policy contributed to the overall record of stability achieved by the deposit insurance system in the 1980s."[26] Evidently, some notions are just too strong to resist.

THE ISSUE "RESOLVED"

For much of the 1980s, the too big to fail concept was an important element in the debates about if and how the regulatory system for depository institutions should be changed. Too big to fail can be examined from many perspectives: semantical, human behavioral, political, even comedic. The underlying reality, however, is that the imminent failure of a large institution, whether in the banking sector of the economy or in some other sector, presents the government with great uncertainties. The possible impacts on economic activity in general, on employment, on related and not-so-related industries are of such magnitudes as to make nonaction by government authorities a difficult course to follow. Hardships are threatened, and governments are in the business of mitigating hardships.

For example, in four notable situations outside the banking industry in the 1970s, the U.S. government found that institutions were in essence too big to fail. In 1971, Congress authorized a $250 million loan guarantee for the aircraft manufacturer Lockheed. The funds were needed to enable the company to complete the development of a commercial—not military—jet, the L–1011 Tri–Star. Government involvement was rationalized on the grounds of Lockheed's importance in the defense industry and on the perceived need to increase competition in the commercial aircraft manufacturing industry.

The desire to maintain competition was also a rationale for the government's rescue of Chrysler Corporation in 1979–80. Another motivating factor was concern about the loss of jobs that a failure would entail. Congress authorized $1.5 billion in government loan guarantees for the car manufacturer. The government aid helped both Lockheed and Chrysler survive their difficulties.

A third instance of too big to fail aid in the 1970s involved a municipality. In 1975, Congress authorized loans of up to $2.3 billion to the tottering New York City. This followed action by the state government establishing an entity, the Municipal Assistance Corporation, to sell long term bonds backed by the state to pay off the city's short term debt. A major rationale for the aid by the state and federal governments was fear and uncertainty about the possible consequences of a default by the city.

And in a more pervasive involvement, Congress acted at various times during the decade to save elements of the railroad industry. In 1970, Congress allowed the Penn Central Railroad to default on private sector loans but then stepped in with $125 million in loan guarantees to permit the failed company to continue operations. Also in 1970, Congress created a semipublic corporation, Amtrak, to operate a nationwide rail passenger service. Amtrak was still receiving federal support in 1997. In 1974–76, Congress provided aid in the form of $1.5 billion in loan guarantees and $2.7 billion in design, start-up, and operating costs to form Consolidated Rail Corporation—Conrail—which was a combination of seven bankrupt railroads in the Northeast and Midwest. Congress authorized the sale of Conrail in 1986.

The point is that too big to fail is not just a banking industry problem. It surfaces whenever any large institution in the economy encounters difficulties. Regardless of whether one believes that government action is warranted in a particular case, one has to concede that government action will at least be considered. And although the result of government action may appear unfair from the standpoint of smaller institutions, the appearance of unfairness will only be an impediment, not an absolute barrier, to a publicly funded effort at resolution. What was unique about the banking industry in the 1980s, and what brought too big to fail to the fore, was, first, the prolonged escalation of the troubles and, second, the existence of a government structure that seemed in the eyes of some to provide too easy an avenue for government action. That government structure also afforded a target for rantings about the apparent unfairness.

Finally, in 1991, Congress was persuaded that curtailment of the too big to fail "policy" was called for. Banking industry troubles reached their zenith in that year and led to enactment of the Federal Deposit Insurance Corporation Improvement Act (FDICIA). Among the provisions of that law, which as a general matter expanded the oversight tools of the banking regulators, is a systemic risk exception to the least cost requirement. Section 141 of FDICIA requires the FDIC to handle failed or failing banks in the least costly manner. Under the systemic risk exception, the least cost requirement can be overridden if the Board of Directors of the FDIC, the Board of Governors of the Federal Reserve System, and the secretary of the treasury (in consultation with the president) determines that compliance in a particular instance "would have serious adverse effects on economic conditions or financial stability."[27]

The banking industry has staged a remarkable recovery since 1991—although not necessarily because of FDICIA—and no situation has arisen in which the systemic risk exception might have been considered. Thus it remains untested. At a less practical, more academic level, an intriguing question tempts the students of "policy." Did the enactment of the least cost requirement and the systemic risk exception end a too big to fail "policy," or was the "policy" bequeathed an official existence? On the one hand, is the argument that Section 141's systemic risk exception is not, after all, mandatory. The regulators are not required to deal with a failing large bank in a manner different from the manner in which they would deal with a failing small or medium-size bank. They merely have the option to do so if they believe the situation warrants it.

But then there is the view exemplified in a 1996 study for the Bank Administration Institute.[28] The study recommended, as part of a long term effort to privatize deposit insurance, that the "residual" too big to fail policy be eliminated. Although FDICIA in theory codified the doctrine that no bank is too big to fail, many bankers at smaller organizations look at the systemic risk exception and are not persuaded. Consequently, they believe, all doubt should be removed by removing the exception.

An even more forceful opinion has been expressed by, perhaps surprisingly, the president and chief executive officer (CEO) of a large banking organization. Richard M. Kovacevich of Norwest Corporation has also advanced an insurance privatization proposal.[29] Writing in 1995, four years after the enactment of FDICIA, Mr. Kovacevich stated: "privatizing the FDIC would eliminate the need for intrusive regulation justified by the current open-ended 'too-big-to-fail' coverage of the government's insurance program." If the post–FDICIA deposit insurance program is "open-ended," one hesitates to contemplate what Mr. Kovacevich thought of the pre–FDICIA program.

Thus too big to fail continues to hover over the never-ending debate about the role of government in shaping the structure of the U.S. banking industry. The concept is not in the forefront as it was for much of the 1980s. But as long as perfect justice remains a chimera, as long as some individuals and organizations are, for one reason or another, treated differently by the law, too big to fail will provide a rallying point for seekers of alternative ways of doing things.

NOTES

1. "Isaac Reassesses Continental Bailout," *American Banker*, July 31, 1989, p. 6.

2. Irvine H. Sprague, *Bailout* (New York: Basic Books, Inc., 1986), p. 113.

3. Ibid., pp. 152–153. In a discussion on the McLaughlin Group talk show on May 4, Mr. Novak, noting the possibility that the Federal Reserve System would loosen the money supply, stated such an action was likely "only in the event of a bank failure, maybe something like the Continental Illinois in Chicago."

4. Section 11(f) of the Federal Deposit Insurance (FDI) Act, 12 U.S.C. §1821(f). Paying off insured depositors can be accomplished by the FDIC directly or by making the deposit available through an agent bank. The latter alternative, called by the FDIC an insured deposit transfer, has been used frequently since 1983.

5. The FDIC's authority to arrange for the acquisition of all or a portion of a failed or failing bank is broad and covers a variety of legal transaction types. The authority is codified at §13(c)(2) of the FDI Act, 12 U.S.C. §1823(c)(2). The term "deposit assumption" has been the FDIC *Annual Report* phrase used to cover such acquisitions, with the term "purchase and assumption" (P&A) being applied to the most prevalent type of deposit assumption. See David Holland, "Bank Failure Terminology: The Forest for the Trees," *Golembe Reports* (Vol. 1991–9), for a discussion of the confusing world of bank failure terminology.

6. The authority to infuse funds into an existing institution is set forth at §13(c)(1) of the FDI Act, 12 U.S.C. §1823(c)(1). Although provided to the FDIC in 1950, the authority did not receive its first use until 1970. Its use since then has been infrequent.

7. 12 U.S.C. Section 1823 (c)(4). Somewhat confusingly, the provision also prohibits the FDIC, with an exception regarding P&A transactions, from protecting uninsured deposits or other liabilities if such an action would increase losses to the insurance fund. The P&A exception is that an acquirer of a failed institution may acquire uninsured deposit liabilities as

long as the insurance fund would not incur a loss greater than the loss that would have been incurred in a liquidation.

8.   See Federal Deposit Insurance Corporation, *Mandate for Change* (Washington, D.C., 1987), p. 112.

9.   From 1951 to 1991, the FDIC was constrained by a "cost" test in deciding how to deal with a failed or failing institution. Originating as a commitment by the FDIC chairman to a congressional subcommittee in 1951 (see FDIC, *The First Fifty Years*, 1984, pp. 86–87), the test was codified in §111 of the 1982 Garn-St Germain Act, which stated in part that the FDIC could provide no merger assistance "in an amount in excess of that . . . necessary to save the cost of liquidating" a bank. An "essentiality" exception was triggered if the FDIC determined that continued operation of the bank was essential to provide adequate banking services to the community. As noted in the text, FDICIA in 1991 replaced the cost test with a least-cost test.

10.   Federal Deposit Insurance Corporation, Division of Finance, *Failed Bank Cost Analysis, 1986–1992*, p. 4.

11.   See the earlier discussion on the FDIC's modified payout experiment in 1983–84.

12.   Federal Deposit Insurance Corporation, *Annual Report, 1984*, p. 4.

13.   Sprague, p. 256. The major bank resolutions described in Mr. Sprague's book are Unity Bank of Boston, 1971; Bank of the Commonwealth, Detroit, 1971; First Pennsylvania Bank, 1980; Penn Square Bank, 1982; Seattle First National Bank, 1982; and Continental Illinois, 1984.

14.   "Inquiry into Continental Illinois Corp. and Continental Illinois National Bank," *Hearings before the Subcommittee on Financial Institutions Supervision, Regulation and Insurance of the Committee on Banking, Finance and Urban Affairs*, 98th Cong., 2nd Sess., September 18, 19, and October 4, 1984.

15.   Tim Carrington, "U. S. Won't Let 11 Biggest Banks in Nation Fail," September 20, 1984, p. 2, sec. 1.

16.   R. Charles Moyer and Robert E. Lamy, " 'Too Big to Fail': Rationale, Consequences, and Alternatives," *Business Economics* (July 1992), p. 19.

17.   Ibid., p. 21.

18.   Tim Carrington, "Panel Questions FDIC Warnings In Bank Bailout," October 5, 1984, p. 6., sec 1.

19.   L. William Seidman, Testimony on "Deposit Insurance Revision and Financial Services Restructuring," before the Senate Banking Committee, July 31, 1990. The author was personally involved in the preparation of this testimony and attributes the contradiction largely to the time-honored government practice of writing by group.

20.   *Hearing before the Subcommittee on Economic Stabilization of the House Committee on Banking, Finance and Urban Affairs*, 102nd Cong., 1st Sess., Serial No. 102-31, May 9, 1991.

21.   Ibid., p. 1.

22.   Ibid., p. 6.

23.   Ibid.

24.   Ibid., p. 18.

25.   The four instances in which the essentiality exception had been invoked over the previous five years were (1) First National Bank & Trust Co., Oklahoma City, Oklahoma, assets of $1.6 billion, 1986; (2) First Republic Bank, Dallas, Texas, assets of $32.9 billion, 1988; (3) MCorp, Houston, Texas, Assets of $15.8 billion, 1989; (4) Bank of New England, Boston, Massachusetts, assets of $22.9 billion, 1991. Prior to the enactment of the Garn-St Germain Act in 1982, a somewhat different essentiality requirement had existed: use by the FDIC of the open bank assistance power, which had been authorized by Congress in 1950, required a finding that the bank was essential to its community.

26. Federal Deposit Insurance Corporation, *History of the Eighties; Lessons for the Future,* 1997, p. 42.

27. 2 U.S.C. §1823(c)(4)(G).

28. Bank Administration Institute and McKinsey & Company, Inc., *Building Better Banks: The Case for Performance-Based Regulation* (1996).

29.   Richard M. Kovacevich, "Deposit Insurance: It's Time to Cage the Monster," *Banking Policy Report* (November 20, 1995), p. 1.

5

Texans Do It Bigger

Outsiders often perceive Texans as prone to claims of excess: the hottest chili, the prettiest women, the handsomest men, the meanest dogs, the longest snakes, the most variable weather. Well, in the 1980s, Texans could lay claim to another excess: the failingest banks. Indeed, without Texas the banking shakeout of the 1980s and early 1990s would have been much less severe. Texas, however, put the situation in a different dimension, raising to almost a crisis level what otherwise are adequately characterized as "difficulties" or "troubles."

As it entered the 1980s, Texas was a leading example of the flawed condition of much of the nation's banking structure. Severe geographic restraints on banking had led to an independent bank—or two or three—in practically every locale. Multi-office institutions were virtually nonexistent. The Texas constitution of 1876 had prohibited bank branching, and this remained the law until 1986.[1] In 1980, Texas was one of 11 unit banking states—states that allowed almost no degree of branch banking. As a consequence, Texas, with 6.2 percent of the nation's population and 6.4 percent of the nation's banking assets, was home to an inordinate proportion of the nation's 14,422 banks: 1,467, or 10.2 percent. Texas had one bank for every 9,700 individuals, compared to a nationwide ratio of one bank for every 15,800 individuals.[2]

In 1970, in a reluctant and only partial nod to economic reality, the state had authorized the bank holding company structure as an expansion possibility. Texas bankers who wanted to grow rushed to take advantage of the new opportunity. At year-end 1970, Texas had four bank holding companies owning a total of 14 banks, which accounted for 7.5 percent of the state's commercial bank assets. A year later, the number of holding companies had jumped to 108. They controlled 142 banks holding 47.4 percent of commercial bank assets. By the end of 1980, the number of holding companies was 256. Forty-four of these were multibank holding companies controlling a total of 334 banks holding 64.5 percent of commercial bank assets.[3] Thus bankers had found a way to overcome the economically debilitating barrier of no branch banking, but it was an inefficient way. It required the setting up of a separate bank, individually capitalized and with its own board of directors, at every location where an organization desired to have a banking facility. From the perspective of centralized control of costs and activities, a holding company structure containing a number of subsidiary banks presents a considerably greater challenge than a branch banking structure.

No institution emerged as the undisputed top dog in the rush among Texas banks to the holding company structure. Instead, by the early 1980s a number of competitors were slugging it out. Headquartered in Dallas were three behemoths— RepublicBank Corporation, Mercantile Texas Corporation (later MCorp), and InterFirst Corporation—and the smaller BancTexas Group, Inc. In Houston were Texas Commerce Bancshares, Allied Bancshares, and First City Bancorporation. Texas American Bancshares was based in Forth Worth. And National Bancshares of Texas and Cullen/Frost Bankers were in San Antonio. Of these 10 institutions, only Cullen/Frost was to survive the travails ahead without outside assistance.

WHAT GOES UP . . .

Prodded by the Arab-Israeli War of October 1973, the Organization of Petroleum Exporting Countries (OPEC), moved in the last months of that year on long-discussed plans to increase substantially the financial returns on the vital natural resource possessed by its members. The official price of a barrel of Arabian Light, the benchmark Saudi crude, went from $2.90 in mid-1973 to $11.65 in December, a fourfold increase.[4] Moreover, in late October, largely in response to U.S. aid to Israel during the conflict, Arab oil exporters, led by Saudi Arabia, had begun an embargo on oil sales to Western nations. The principal target of the harshest provisions of the embargo was the United States. The embargo lasted only a few months, but it served to emphasize the very tight supply-demand relationship that had developed concerning oil and was a specter hanging over the remainder of the decade. Because of the relative paucity of oil supplies worldwide in relation to demand during this time, the pricing actions of OPEC were mirrored by other suppliers. For example, West Texas intermediate crude oil jumped from $4.31 a barrel in December 1973 to $10.11 a barrel in January 1974. The average U.S. domestic crude-oil refiner acquisition cost in 1973 was $4.17 a barrel. In 1974, it was $7.18 a barrel, an almost twofold increase.[5] Following the initial jump, both OPEC and non-OPEC prices trended generally upward until the end of the decade when the replacement of the Shah of Iran by a fundamentalist regime and the resulting turmoil, including the takeover of the U.S. embassy and the holding of American hostages for over a year, caused another spurt. The OPEC price went from $13 a barrel in 1979 to $34 in 1981.[6] The U.S. domestic crude-oil refiner acquisition cost rose over the same period from $14.27 a barrel to $34.33.[7]

The oil price increases fed and exacerbated other volatile situations and developments, including the breakdown of the international fixed rate currency exchange system and the inflationary tide set loose by U.S. monetary and fiscal policies in the 1960s, to make the 1970s a time of general economic anxiety. A recession began in the United States in November 1973. It lasted for 16 months, until March 1975. Gross domestic product declined 4.1 percent, the largest decline of any post–World War II recession, and unemployment reached 9.0 percent.

But Texas largely escaped the economic anxiety and the troubles of the decade. The state possessed in abundance the item whose relative scarcity was a cause of the problems elsewhere: oil. The energy industry had long accounted for a sizeable slice of the Texas economy. The actions of Middle Eastern sheiks increased dramatically the value of what lay below the soil of Texas and its neighbors and fanned the fires of capitalism with a gale-force wind. The number of rotary oil rigs operating in the United States rose from fewer than 1,000 in 1971 to over 2,200 in 1978.[8] From such direct, immediate effects of the price increases, economic activity spread to supplying and supporting, and parasitic, endeavors. The real estate industry particularly benefitted, as did the providers of funds—banks and S&Ls. The second price spurt at the turn of the decade, the spurt due to the Iranian turmoil, raised the level of activity from the exuberant to the frenetic. An indication of the increased enthusiasm was a further growth in the number of rotary oil rigs from the 2,200 of 1978 to over 4,500 at the end of 1981.[9]

As a result of the application of human effort to nature's bounty, Texans not only avoided the economic travails of the 1970s: they prospered. Between 1973 and 1983, industrial production rose 20 percent nationwide but doubled in Texas. The state's per capita income rose from 11 percent below the nation's average in 1973 to 2 percent above the average in 1980.[10] Spurred by single-digit vacancy rates in the major metropolitan areas for much of the decade, the real estate industry commenced a building binge. In banking, the assets of Texas banks reached a growth rate peak of 20.5 percent in 1980. The national rate for that year was 8.6 percent.[11] Shifts in bank lending portfolios show where the growth was occurring. Construction and land development loans, a category that includes loans to, among others, commercial real-estate developers and oil and gas producers, increased from 2.1 percent of the assets of Texas banks in 1976 to 4.1 percent in 1980 to 8.3 percent in 1984. For another category, commercial and industrial loans, which includes loans to, among others, oil and gas producers, the increase was from 20.7 percent of the assets of the state's banks in 1978 to 27.8 percent in 1982.[12]

The law of supply and demand that had ignited the Texas economic fires was now ready to show its other side, however. Worldwide, the supply of oil had increased, and demand was falling in response to the higher prices. From 62.6 million barrels per day in 1979, world consumption of oil fell to 52.5 million barrels in 1983.[13] The first break in the upward spiral of prices came in 1981. In both inflation-adjusted and nominal terms, the dollar-denominated price of oil declined. The initial decline was not overly large—U.S. domestic crude-oil refiner acquisition cost went from $34.33 per barrel in 1981 to $31.22 in 1982 to $28.87 in 1983[14]—but it was devastating to an industry geared to only an upward movement. The number of rigs operating in Texas fell 51 percent between

December 1981 and April 1983, and employment in oil and gas field extraction dropped 20 percent. Between December 1981 and early 1984, employment in the oil field machinery industry dropped 50 percent.[15]

But the rapid change in the fortunes of and outlook for the oil and gas industry was not enough to bring the boom mentality in Texas and the surrounding area to a halt. To be sure, casualties occurred among those with immediate and deep ties to the industry. The instigator of Continental Illinois' downfall, Penn Square Bank of Oklahoma, failed in July 1982, a victim of essentially speculative energy-related lending. Depositors were paid off by the FDIC. In August 1982, the troubled Abilene National Bank, Abilene, Texas, with assets of $450 million, was acquired by Mercantile Texas Corporation, the predecessor of MCorp. The FDIC provided assistance for the transaction, as it did for the acquisition in October of Oklahoma National Bank and Trust Company by the First National Bank and Trust Company of Oklahoma City. In October of the following year, 1983, The First National Bank of Midland, with $1.4 billion in assets, failed. Its deposit liabilities were assumed by a subsidiary of RepublicBank Corporation. Between 1982 and the end of 1987, the banks serving the heart of the West Texas oil patch were generally pummeled. All four independent banks in Midland and three of the four independent banks in Odessa failed.[16]

Banks with relatively less exposure to the oil and gas industry, however, thought little of retrenchment or defensive action. The imperative was to continue the growth and profitability of the recent past. Not perceiving imminent difficulties, these banks merely shifted their focus. Real estate became the principal scene of the action. Deregulated S&Ls added to the frenzy. The Depository Institutions Deregulation and Monetary Control Act of 1980 expanded the authority of federally chartered S&Ls to make acquisition, development, and construction loans. The Garn-St Germain Depository Institutions Act of 1982 allowed federal S&Ls to invest up to 40 percent of their assets in commercial mortgage loans. Texas was even more permissive, opening up, in the words of one study, "virtually any activity to its S&Ls."[17] As noted in Chapter 3, a certain laxity in supervision accompanied the expansion of S&L powers. This laxity enabled many S&L owners, both in Texas and elsewhere, to exercise their expanded powers with more enthusiasm than discretion and a few to venture into areas of outright criminality.[18]

Real estate–related loans became a buyers' market. Lenders fell over themselves to shove money at builders and developers. Lending standards deteriorated. "Mini-perms"—loans for up to five-years in length and generally with floating rates—replaced the fixed-rate permanent take-out mortgages that had previously been the standard. Mini-perms first became prominent in the period of high interest rates in the late 1970s, but they remained a common practice even when rates declined in the early 1980s. Lenders using mini-perms often became less concerned about a project's long term viability. Only being committed for the short term, lenders only looked to the short term. Requirements for builders and developers to obtain leasing commitments from prospective tenants were relaxed. Borrowers' balance sheets replaced the need for putting actual equity into projects. Loans for the acquisition of raw land for development became difficult to distinguish from loans for the acquisition of land for speculation.[19] Looking back, one former Texas banker described the situation thusly:

The competition was fierce, and it was apparent that, if we were to compete, we had to conform to the new lending practices. Accordingly, we relented to the pressures of the market place and adopted the more relaxed standards that had become commonplace in the industry.

TAB [Texas American Bancshares] wasn't unique: virtually every major real estate lender in the country conformed. Bankers across the U.S. let competition, the quest for earnings, the need to show successive quarterly increases and 15 percent annual increases, and pressures from the investment community dictate actions.[20]

The real estate binge did not take long to produce a state of overfedness. For the years 1977 through 1983, the office vacancy rate for the four Texas cities of Austin, Dallas, Houston, and San Antonio was never above 10 percent. But from 4.9 percent in 1983, the rate shot up to 11.5 percent in 1984, 15.4 percent in 1985, 24.8 percent in 1986, and 29.7 percent in 1987.[21]

Two events accelerated and exacerbated the approaching debacle. OPEC had been trying to maintain the price structure of the oil market by curtailing production. Non-OPEC oil, alternative energy sources, and conservation measures were increasingly frustrating the strategy, however. The shift in power from petroleum suppliers to petroleum users that had begun early in the decade was continuing, and the cartel's market share was eroding. First Saudi Arabia and then in late 1985 the remainder of OPEC abandoned the effort to maintain prices, and commenced to target volume. The effect on prices was abrupt and drastic. The average Texas oil price plummeted from $30.00 a barrel in December 1985 to $9.75 in April 1986.[22] The Texas oil industry and its suppliers were hit hard, and their lenders were not far behind in feeling the pain. The second event was enactment of the Tax Reform Act of 1986. In that act, the U.S. Congress curtailed significantly the ability of taxpayers to deduct losses generated by passive investment activities. This action reduced the attractiveness of real estate as an investment and contributed substantially to declines in real estate values.

THEY MAY NOT HAVE BEEN DOMINOS, BUT THEY SURE FELL LIKE DOMINOS

Between 1982 and 1987, nonperforming assets as a percentage of total assets of Texas banks increased from 1.75 percent to 6.6 percent. In 1986, the state's banking industry experienced its first negative return, -0.49 percent. For 1987, ROA fell to -1.40 percent.[23] The number of Texas bank failures rose from 12 in 1985 to 26 in 1986, 50 in 1987, 113 in 1988, and 133 in 1989, which was the peak.[24] But as eyebrow-raising as such statistics may be, they are inadequate in conveying the extent of the damage to the Texas banking industry, damage both to institutions themselves and to the macho, self-reliant, image that Texans had of their state and its activities.

With little doubt, the most significant statistic for this purpose is that 9 of the 10 largest banking organizations in the state in the early 1980s did not survive the turmoil as independent institutions. The one survivor was Cullen/Frost Bankers. Two organizations—Texas Commerce Bancshares and Allied Bancshares—were acquired by out-of-state bank holding companies in voluntary transactions with no government aid. The remaining seven organizations, or their remnants, also eventually ended up in the hands of out-of-state banking organizations, but the journeys were often tortuous. An interesting minor question is, which was more humiliating for Texas bankers: to go of their own accord into the hands of out-of-staters, or to be poked, prodded, cajoled, or otherwise forced there by unfeeling denizens of the federal government?

But before the big guns of the Texas banking industry—the Texas Nine—encountered their fates, two sizeable institutions in neighboring Oklahoma succumbed to the growing troubles. In the summer of 1986, just six months after the sharp reduction in oil prices at the beginning of the year, the First National Bank and Trust Company of Oklahoma City, which in 1982 had acquired the ailing Oklahoma National Bank and Trust Company with FDIC assistance, was itself in extremis. With assets of $1.6 billion, First National was Oklahoma's third largest bank. The FDIC provided assistance for its acquisition, after closure, by First Interstate Bancorp of Los Angeles, California. The second largest Oklahoma institution floundered in August. In that month, the FDIC granted $130 million in open bank assistance to a subsidiary of BancOklahoma, with assets of $2.7 billion the second largest banking organization in the state. All told in 1986, 16 Oklahoma banks failed and 1 was given open bank assistance.

The tales of the nine Texas institutions stretch over a period of eight years and collectively are not easy to follow. Several of the tales cover just one event. Others, however, contain multiple, sometimes overlapping, chapters. This plus the banking industry's long-existing penchant for similar institutional names can make untangling what happened to the Texas banking industry between 1986 and 1993 a most challenging task.

Texas Commerce Bancshares

Texas Commerce Bancshares's tale is among the more straightforward. With assets of $20 billion at year-end 1985, it was the state's fourth largest bank holding company. On December 15, 1986, its acquisition by Chemical New York Corporation, the parent of Chemical Bank, was announced. Texas Commerce was not in immediate trouble, but it was suffering. Nonperforming assets were rapidly rising, moving from 3.6 percent of loans and foreclosed real estate in the first quarter of 1985 to 6.5 percent in the third quarter of 1986. Earnings through September 1986 were half of what they had been a year earlier. Real estate loans were approximately 31 percent of total loans, not a matter for comfort given the deteriorating real estate market.[25] Some analysts viewed the transaction as a bargain for Texas Commerce shareholders, who were to receive value of approximately $35 a share for stock having a realistic book value in the neighborhood of $20 a share. Other analysts wondered why Chemical would seek to enter such a troubled economy. Chemical, however, was undoubtedly looking to the long term. Moreover, it established some protections for itself. Part of the purchase price paid to Texas Commerce shareholders was a class of stock tied to Texas Commerce's future earnings. Another part of the purchase price was stock in a new "bad bank" formed to hold and dispose of a portion of Texas Commerce's non-performing assets.

The transaction, the first major entry by an out-of-state organization, was a shock to Texans, especially so because the chairman of Texas Commerce, Ben F. Love, had for many years been a prominent and enthusiastic "Texas-firster," a foremost booster of the state. The dean of the graduate business school at Rice University probably expressed the things-will-never-be-the-same reaction of many Texans: "There is a strong symbolic message in this. The notion of the Republic of Texas and the idea that we can do everything all by ourselves have gone by the boards, and this merger is going to force people to face up to it. Given the economics in the state, it's inevitable that we just can't go it alone any longer."[26]

RepublicBank Corporation and InterFirst Corporation

With barely a day to digest the Texas Commerce-Chemical announcement, Texans received another heaping bit of news. Crosstown rivals—the town being Dallas—RepublicBank Corporation and InterFirst Corporation were merging to form First Republic Bancorporation. With year-end assets of $23.2 billion and $22.1 billion, respectively, the institutions were the first and third largest in the state. Combined, they would be the nation's thirteenth largest banking organization. Both were in a weakened condition with InterFirst being the more so, in part because of participations in energy lending with the First National Bank of Midland, which had failed in 1983. The merger had at least the tacit encouragement of federal banking regulators. The combining of two weak banks, however, did not prove to be a viable strategy. Less than a year after the consummation of the transaction in the second quarter of 1987, First Republic was suffering a very public deterioration. It lost $658.8 million for the year, and its nonperforming assets were 15.9 percent of loans and foreclosed assets.[27]

In March 1988, the FDIC, to stem the electronic withdrawal of deposits by other Texas banks from the First Republic system, advanced a $1 billion loan to First Republic's two largest banks and provided assurances of full protection to all bank depositors and bank creditors.[28] The protection, however, did not extend to funding among the banks within the First Republic holding company system or to holding company obligations. The loan effectively put First Republic within the tender clutches of the federal banking regulators. Absent a miraculous recovery of unprecedented speed, the outcome was inevitable, and its timing largely under the control of the FDIC. After lining up North Carolina's NCNB Corporation to take over the remains, the FDIC in late July pulled the plug by not renewing the loan. This rendered the lead bank "nonviable," in the words of the FDIC's *Annual Report*.[29] Resulting losses on intrabank financing and loan guarantees rendered in turn the other banks in the holding company insolvent, thus giving the FDIC grounds to take over the entire system. This would not be the last time that the regulators gained disposition authority over most of the assets of a Texas bank holding company by precipitating an insolvency contagion.[30] On July 29, 1988, the

FDIC created a bridge bank to be managed by NCNB Corporation. The bridge bank, NCNB Texas National Bank, received the assets and liabilities of the 40 banks that were closed, but did not assume the obligations of the holding company. NCNB Corporation and the FDIC completed a permanent recapitalization in November, amounting to $1.05 billion. Initially, 20 percent of the amount was provided by NCNB, and the remaining 80 percent by the FDIC.

Allied Bancshares

On May 21, 1987, Allied Bancshares became only the second of the Texas Nine to go directly and voluntarily into the hands of out-of-staters. On that date, Allied, with assets at year-end 1986 of $9.9 billion and headquartered in Houston, announced that it would be acquired by First Interstate Bancorp of Los Angeles, California, the nation's ninth largest bank holding company. The transaction was similar to the Texas Commerce-Chemical transaction in that future earnings and a "bad" bank provided some protections to First Interstate: the compensation to Allied shareholders was dependent in part on the acquired institution's future performance; and a portion of Allied's nonperforming loans were spun off into a workout bank.

BancTexas

Dallas-headquartered BancTexas, with $1.8 billion in assets at year-end 1985, was actually the first of the Texas Nine to earn the term "failed," its initial government aid coming after the RepublicBank-Interfirst merger to form First Republic Bancorporation in 1987 but before that resulting organization's fall into the regulators' hands in 1988. BancTexas was acquired by an investor group, the Hallwood Group, Inc., in July 1987. The FDIC provided $150 million in open bank assistance. BancTexas had grown rapidly from 1980 to 1983, when its problems began to mount, slowly at first. The decline in its condition accelerated in 1986 in concert with the accumulating devastation of the real estate market and the pounding the Texas economy was taking from the fall in oil prices at the beginning of the year. From December 1985 to June 1987, BancTexas's nonperforming real estate assets increased from 1.1 percent to 8.5 percent of total assets.[31]

As a rescuer, the Hallwood Group did not prove to be a fortuitous choice. In early 1988, the FDIC also granted the Group $295 million in open bank assistance to acquire control of the Alliance Bancorporation of Anchorage, Alaska, the successor of two troubled Alaska banks. Both BancTexas and Alliance Bancorporation continued to deteriorate and eventually both "failed" a second time. Alliance Bancorporation's subsidiary bank was closed in April 1989, and its deposits and healthy assets were assumed by another Alaskan institution. BancTexas's principal subsidiary was closed on January 26, 1990, and its deposits and healthy assets were assumed by a subsidiary of Hibernia Corporation of Louisiana. The story was not over, however. Louisiana's economy had not received the bludgeoning that the Texas economy had experienced, but the energy industry did play an important role in Louisiana, and the state was sorely bruised. Shortly after the acquisition of BancTexas, Hibernia joined the walking wounded, posting a loss of $165 million for 1991. In early 1992, Hibernia sold its Texas banking operations to Comerica of Detroit, Michigan.

In February 1989, as the Hallwood Group's investments in BancTexas and Alliance were unraveling, the *American Banker* published an article identifying what it termed "three mistakes" regarding the transactions.[32] First, "the FDIC broke one of its own rules, a requirement that assistance transactions should restore recipient institutions to economic viability." In both transactions, too many bad loans and foreclosed properties were left on the books and not offset by the capital infusions. Second, the transactions were premised on the expectation that the economies of Texas and Alaska would recover faster than they were in fact recovering. Third, the assistance by the FDIC was a one-time fixed amount with no provision for additional aid if the institutions' conditions continued to deteriorate. The FDIC declined comment for the article.

First City Bancorporation

For the FDIC, a serious attempt at identifying mistakes in its Texas efforts was well in the future. In the meantime, events were offering little time for reflection. In September 1987, the agency announced an open bank assistance agreement of almost $1 billion—$970 million, to be precise—for the acquisition of First City Bancorporation of Houston. First City had assets of approximately $11 billion at year-end 1987 and 59 banking subsidiaries. It had lost $406 million in 1986, and its prospects were dismal. The transaction was completed in April 1988. The acquirer was A. Robert Abboud, an odd choice in the view of some observers.[33] Mr. Abboud's resume included ousters in 1980 as chief executive officer of First National Bank of Chicago and in 1984 as president of Occidental Petroleum.

Taking a cue from the Texas Commerce-Chemical and Allied Bancshares-First Interstate private sector transactions, the FDIC had a "bad bank" established to manage First City's nonperforming assets. First City's fate was tied in part to the "bad bank," however, as the latter provided senior notes to First City banks in exchange for funds. Recovery on the nonperforming assets was below expectations, and in the third quarter of 1990 the banks took a $77 million write-off on the notes.[34] This loss added to the problems created by the aggressive, risky strategy pursued by Mr. Abboud. To offset the sluggishness of the Texas recovery and continued deterioration in the portfolios of some of First City's banks, Mr. Abboud threw the organization into the fields of highly levered transactions (HLTs) and international lending. The results were not unpredictable. Losses for 1990 and the first quarter of 1991 were almost $230 million, and Mr. Abboud was shone the door.

His successors tried to stave off the federal regulators, but to no avail. Armed with a cross-guarantee provision provided by Congress in the Financial Institutions Reform, Recovery, and Enforcement Act of 1989, the regulators engineered First City's failure on October 30, 1992.[35] Two of First City's 20 bank subsidiaries[36] were closed by their chartering authorities. The FDIC then assessed the other banks for the losses of the first two. These losses rendered the remaining banks insolvent, and consequently they were closed, victims of an insolvency contagion. Twenty bridge banks were established to assume the deposits and assets of the 20 closed banks. For 16 of the closed banks, the better capitalized ones, all deposits were transferred to the bridge banks. In the cases of the remaining four closed banks, uninsured deposits totaling approximately $260 million were not transferred. The FDIC provided the uninsured depositors in these four banks with initial payments equal to 80 percent of the accounts. In January 1993, the FDIC sold the 20 bridge banks to 12 different financial institutions, including Texas Commerce Bancshares, now owned by Chemical Banking Corporation of New York.

First City's saga was not over, however. The usual lawsuits challenged the FDIC's actions, but perhaps with a bit more vehemence than usual. Mr. Abboud's successors believed they had been on the brink of a private sector recapitalization of the institution.[37] First City shareholders, creditors, and management consequently felt particularly aggrieved by the FDIC's intrusion. A suit by First City against the Comptroller of the Currency, the FDIC, and the Texas Banking Commissioner asked for approximately $1 billion in ordinary damages and up to $2 billion in punitive damages. Although normally not shy about defending its actions regarding closed banks in court, the FDIC had to contend with an unpleasant fact. Instead of the $500 million dollar loss that the agency initially predicted it would incur as a result the seizure of First City, an embarrassing surplus, or "profit," appeared likely.[38] Estimates of the surplus ranged from the FDIC's own $60 million to as much as $500 million. With this prod, the FDIC's litigiousness seemed to give way to a more receptive attitude about settling the case. A settlement agreement was reached in June 1994 and finalized the following May. One result of the settlement was that uninsured depositors who initially were given only 80 cents on the dollar received full restitution.

MCorp

The regulators' ability to bring down First City through an insolvency contagion owed much to the difficulty they had with MCorp in 1989, before the passage in August of that year of the FIRREA and its cross-guarantee provision. In fact, the MCorp experience was what prompted the regulators to seek the cross-guarantee provision from Congress.[39] MCorp's demise was not the multistage, multiyear affair of the First City and BancTexas downfalls. The Dallas-based bank holding company, which had assets of $22.6 billion at year-end 1985, first experienced an annual loss in 1986. It continued to post losses until the closure of 20 of its 25 bank subsidiaries in March 1989. The only federal intervention of consequence during this period was a $1 billion loan from the Federal Reserve discount window in November 1988. No ineffectual public or private sector restructurings postponed, or accelerated, the end.

MCorp approached the coming federal takeover with a desire to keep as much as it could from the clutches of the federal regulators. Its strategy was to use the holding company organization aggressively, keeping funds in the smaller sound banks or at the holding company level and out of the troubled banks, and avoiding as much as possible the interbank lending that would enable the regulators to bring down the entire organization through an insolvency contagion. Naturally, the regulators did not think much of such a strategy and strove to force the holding company to support the weaker banks. The source of strength doctrine was what the regulators, led by the Federal Reserve, relied upon. This doctrine held that holding companies were supposed to be sources of strength for the banks they controlled. But the doctrine ran up against the legal responsibilities of the holding company directors, who had an obligation to do what was best for the holding company as a whole. If this meant allowing some banks within the holding company to fail, so be it in the view of the directors. Complicating the situation was the fact that each bank also had a board of directors responsible for doing what was best for the bank. In some cases, an individual was a director of both the holding company and a subsidiary bank.

FDIC Chairman Seidman's view of the outcome was thus: "The holding company, moving its funds around to keep them beyond the reach of the FDIC, allowed its banks to become insolvent and tossed them to the FDIC to pick up their losses and then held on to the strong ones."[40] The regulators were in fact able to get most of the MCorp organization. Only 5 of MCorp's 25 banks escaped the closures by the OCC in March 1989. The FDIC constructed a bridge bank from the 20 closed institutions. The bridge bank was acquired by Banc One Corporation of Columbus, Ohio, in July 1989. Ultimately, however, MCorp's strategy received a judicial seal of approval. When most of the dust had settled from the subsequent litigation, the holding company and its good, nonseized banks remained as viable private-sector institutions with a substantial amount of cash that the FDIC was not able to use to help offset the loss of more than $2 billion it sustained in the transaction. In short, the Federal Reserve's source of strength doctrine did not override, at least prior to FIRREA, the duties of holding company directors to act in the best interest of the holding company as a whole.

Texas American Bancshares and National Bancshares of Texas

The remaining two of the Texas Nine were Texas American Bancshares (TAB), with assets of $6.4 billion at year-end 1985 and headquartered in Fort Worth, and National Bancshares of Texas (NBC), with year-end 1987 assets of $2.8 billion and headquartered in San Antonio. TAB and NBC were among the smaller of the Texas Nine. Although experiencing losses from 1986 on, the two banking organizations were not finally dealt with by the federal regulators until 1989, for TAB, and 1990, for NBC. Part of the delay was probably due to the regulators' focus on the problems of the larger institutions. The regulators, however, were by no means unaware of the decline of TAB and NBC. Indeed, the two institutions engaged in protracted negotiations over a period of almost two years with the FDIC, negotiations chronicled by TAB chairman and chief executive officer Joseph E. Grant in a scathing critique of the agency's actions.[41] A merger of TAB and NBC and acquisition of the resulting institution by out-of-state parties with significant financial resources were among the proposals examined. In June 1988, the FDIC indicated a desire to grant assistance for such a scenario, but the various components did not fall into place. Open bank assistance for NBC was announced in July 1989, but again the transaction was not consummated.

In the end, each institution was dealt with separately, and in a closed bank transaction. No open bank assistance intruded to disguise the fact that, in the eyes of the regulators at least, the organizations just outright failed. In July 1989, the FDIC was appointed receiver of the 24 subsidiary banks of TAB. An insolvency contagion helped in the closure of the banks. Unlike MCorp, TAB had been unable to reduce interbank lending to a level that granted a degree of immunity from this tactic of the regulators.[42] A bridge bank was established, and it was acquired by the Deposit Guaranty Bank, Dallas. In 1992, Deposit Guaranty was acquired by Banc One Corporation of Ohio. And as for NBC, in June 1990, 9 of its 12 banks were closed and acquired by NCNB Corporation of North Carolina.

JUDGMENTS

For the period 1980 through 1994, Texas ranked first among the states in both the number of bank failures and the amount of failed bank assets. Five hundred ninety-nine Texas banks failed. This was 37 percent of all U.S. bank failures during the period and 29 percent of Texas banks in existence on December 31, 1979, or chartered during the period. The only other state with failures in triple digits was Oklahoma, where 122 banks failed, less than a quarter of the failures in Texas. The failed Texas banks held $93.1 billion in assets at the time of failure, which was 29 percent of the assets of all U.S. banks that failed during the period. New York was the state with the next greatest amount of failed bank assets: $51.6 billion, or just a little more than half of the assets in failed Texas banks.[43]

The Oil Patch as a whole—Texas, Oklahoma, Louisiana, and the northern component, Alaska—accounted during the period for 49 percent of the total number of failed banks and 34 percent of their assets.[44] The woes of the oil industry and the spillover ravaging of real estate markets in the same locales were a foremost component of the banking industry's traumas in the 1980s.

For the FDIC, the Texas bank failures contributed significantly to the beginning of the fall that was to send the deposit insurance fund into negative numbers. The fund reached $18.3 billion in 1987, its apogee prior to the 1990s. In 1988, the year First Republic's banks were closed and sold to NCNB in an assisted transaction and First City received open bank assistance, the FDIC experienced the first operating loss in its history, and the deposit insurance fund declined to $14.1 billion, its first decline since 1947.[45] Annual declines continued—the balance was $13.2 billion at year-end 1989 and $4 billion at year-end 1990—until the fund bottomed out at a negative $7 billion in 1991.

Could the regulators, particularly the FDIC since the deposit insurer is a focus of this work, have done better in Texas? Joseph E. Grant, who was chairman and CEO of Texas American Bancshares, certainly believed so. In *The Great Texas Banking Crash* he portrayed the FDIC as an agency whose ineptitude was relieved only by its deviousness. He is especially critical of FDIC Chairman Seidman. A few samples of his criticisms are:

> A principal protagonist in this saga was the FDIC, whose autocratic chairman, L. William Seidman, presided over an incredible series of blunders, false starts, and ever-changing agendas in dealing with TAB and NBC. Indeed, in most cases, the policies of the FDIC assured the ultimate failure rather than the resurrection of troubled banks, at tremendous

expense to the FDIC's insurance fund and, thus, to the American taxpayer.[46]

Before leaving, we had the opportunity for a brief stand-up meeting with the FDIC chairman, L. William Seidman, outside his office. His curt manner lived up to its reputation. After introductions, he said coolly, 'Well, good luck.' Then he turned on his heels and abruptly went into his office.[47]

They [the FDIC] can't make up their minds. They tell us one thing one day and something else completely different the next. There is no consistency. Doing business with them is a disaster . . . .

We've met every demand and condition they've imposed, but they've given us no idea of what it would take to make a deal. We're only told what isn't acceptable, not what is . . . .

This was a ludicrous situation. Were all government agencies run in such a willy-nilly, irresponsible fashion? . . .

How could Seidman think our situation wasn't urgent? What rock was he living under?[48]

What an unbelievable mess—as ludicrous as a Keystone Cops slapstick farce. It appeared that, the way this deal was being bungled, we didn't have a chance.

On Tuesday, January 17, the Pohlad camp and the FDIC again confirmed that the ball was in the court of the other.[49]

It was a widely held opinion that Seidman was a man with an oversized ego, who was politically motivated and wanted to expand his power base.[50]

The preceding faux pas by the FDIC cost the insurance fund, and thus the taxpayers, hundreds of millions of dollars. The FDIC found that selecting investors to recapitalize insolvent banks is fraught with the same pitfalls that bankers face in making loans. They made mistakes in the investors they selected; they misjudged the amount of funds required to adequately recapitalize the banks; they grossly underestimated the losses on problem loans; and they failed to anticipate the depth of the real estate depression.

The FDIC's record under Chairman L. William Seidman was no better than that of the bankers and directors of insolvent banks that were sued for imprudence, negligence, and violation of their fiduciary responsibilities.[51]

Grant, however, is certainly not an unbiased observer. After a protracted series of negotiations failed to achieve an open bank resolution, the FDIC closed and sold his banks and threatened him with a lawsuit for damages. The suit was not commenced, and thus Grant was more fortunate than some banking officers and directors who had to pay the FDIC for their alleged negligence. Nevertheless, his experience with the FDIC was not a happy one, and his account needs to be read in that light. Moreover, at times his reasoning is not the paragon of consistency. For example, he praised the FDIC's rescue of Continental Illinois and, from a theoretical standpoint, the bank resolution strategy of open bank assistance. But he criticized the FDIC for providing "100 percent guarantee of deposits over $100,000 at some banks,"[52] which happened in the Continental Illinois case and is a consequence of open bank assistance.

But Grant does make several hard-to-dismiss charges. For one thing, facts certainly support the contention that the FDIC made significant mistakes in its open bank assistance efforts in Texas. The consummated open bank transactions for BancTexas and First City Bancorporation did not succeed. The amount of assistance provided turned out to be insufficient, and the new parties allowed in by the FDIC to operate the assisted institutions were not up to the task. And despite lengthy negotiations, transactions for TAB and NBC were never consummated. In hindsight, the time and personnel resources—both at the institutions and at the FDIC—consumed in the exercise might have been focused on more realistic solutions.

Another argument by Grant that might have considerable validity concerns forbearance and the different treatment of similar situations. In later banking problems in other sections of the country, the regulators, in the view of some observers, took a more lenient approach. Grant concentrates on New England, where, as discussed in Chapter 7, Bank of New England Corporation, the nation's sixteenth largest bank holding company, failed in January 1991, a casualty of the spreading deterioration in commercial real estate markets.[53] The failure, according to Grant, was a wake-up call for bankers, politicians, and regulators.[54] Bankers and politicians mounted an aggressive campaign to have the regulators go easy on New England institutions. Partly as a result of the entreaties and pressure, and perhaps partly in response to a belief that maybe they were indeed a little too hard in Texas, the regulators appeared to be bit less harsh in their bank examinations and a bit more forebearing regarding problems. Banks were closed in New England, but a Texas-like lobbing off of all the leading institutions did not occur.

An *American Banker* article of April 20, 1990, provides examples of the aggressive manner in which New England politicians sought to protect the region's banks.[55] Massachusetts Congressman Joseph P. Kennedy was forming a committee to monitor "the flow of credit" into New England. Serving on the committee would be two other Massachusetts Democratic congressmen, Barney Frank and Richard E. Neal, and the Democratic governor, Michael Dukakis. The governor was quoted as accusing the comptroller of the currency of "enforcing stricter standards in New England than in the rest of the country." Rhode Island Governor Edward D. DiPrete showed that the campaign to counter the federal regulators was bipartisan. A Republican, he was quoted as telling senior White House officials, "there is growing evidence that the regulators have overreacted, and their actions are having the effect of stifling the flow of capital in the region."

Grant provides an example of a sharp contrast between the these New Englanders and political leaders in Texas. He paraphrases a purported statement of Texas Governor Bill Clements: "the banks were broke, they deserved to be broke, and he [Clements] wasn't going to do a damn thing to help them."[56]

Is Grant correct about more forbearance being practiced in problems following the Texas experience? A definitive answer is difficult. Moreover, Texas banking structure was unique, perhaps the nation's foremost locus of excess capacity resulting from many decades of protected markets. Thus an attempt to compare regulatory attitudes and forbearance between Texas and other areas of the nation is the proverbial apples versus oranges problem. Nevertheless, only the most politically naive would dismiss the possibility that the in-your-face efforts of the likes of Joe Kennedy and Mike Dukakis did not have an impact. For the most part, federal banking regulators are too principled to break before the political winds. A little judicious bending is not unknown, however.

Perhaps fairness dictates that FDIC Chairman Seidman, the target of much of Mr. Grant's invective, should be permitted the last word on the Texas banking crash. Somewhat obliquely Mr. Seidman acknowledges an error or so, but his overall assessment paints the FDIC, and himself, as saviors: "Nine out of the state's ten big banks failed or were acquired and hundreds of small ones went under, but the FDIC protected the Texas system from collapse. Fortunately—and perhaps precisely because of what we did—the local problems were contained and did not spread into a national disaster."[57]

NOTES

1.   Joseph M. Grant, *The Great Texas Banking Crash: An Insider's Account* (Austin: University of Texas Press, 1996), pp. 7, 69.

2.   Federal Deposit Insurance Corporation, *Historical Statistics on Banking, 1934–1992*; U.S. Bureau of the Census, *Statistical Abstract of the United States: 1994*.

3.   Board of Governors of the Federal Reserve System: *Banking and Monetary Statistics, 1941–1970*; *Annual Statistical Digest*, various issues.

4.   Daniel Yergen, *The Prize* (New York: Simon & Schuster, 1991), p. 625.

5.   John O'Keefe, "The Texas Banking Crisis: Causes and Consequences 1980–1989," *FDIC Banking Review* (Winter 1990), pp. 6, 17.

6.   Yergen, p. 784.

7.   O'Keefe, pp. 6, 17.

8.   Federal Reserve Bank of Dallas, *1984 Annual Report*, pp. 17, 23.

9.   Ibid., p. 23.

10.   Ibid., p. 21.

11.   O'Keefe, p. 4.

12.   Ibid., p. 7.

13.   Federal Reserve Bank of Dallas, p. 23.

14.   Ibid., p. 17.

15.   Ibid., p. 24.

16.   Grant, p. 26.

17.   National Commission on Financial Institution Reform, Recovery and Enforcement, *Origins and Causes of the S&L Debacle: A Blueprint for Reform* (Washington, D.C., July 1993), p. 40.

18.   See Grant, Chapter 3, for a description of several of the more colorful S&L figures and episodes in Texas.

19.   Ibid., pp. 49–50.

20.   Ibid., p. 51.

21.   O'Keefe, p. 17.

22.   Grant, p. 18.

23.   O'Keefe, pp. 7, 19.

24.   Grant, p. 27. The number of failures fell modestly in 1990 to 103, and drastically in 1991 and 1992 to 31 and 29.

25.   Grant, p. 72.

26.   "Chemical's Purchase of Texas Commerce Marks Reversal of Oil Region's Fortunes," *The Wall Street Journal*, December 17, 1986, Matt Moffett, p. 12, sec.1.

27.   Grant, p. 96.

28. L. William Seidman, *Full Faith and Credit* (New York: Times Books, 1995), p. 151.

29. Federal Deposit Insurance Corporation, *Annual Report, 1988*, p. 10.

30. Use of the insolvency contagion tactic was facilitated when Congress in the Financial Institutions Reform, Recovery, and Enforcement Act of 1989 provided for cross-guarantees among commonly controlled institutions. Under Section 206 of the act, an insured depository institution is liable to the FDIC for losses in connection with the default of, or assistance given by the FDIC to, a commonly controlled institution.

31. O'Keefe, p. 27.

32. Steve Klinkerman, "Case Studies: How Not to Rescue a Bank," *American Banker*, February 2, 1989, p. 1.

33. See, for example, Grant, p. 245.

34. Ibid., p. 246.

35. Section 206, codified at 12 U.S.C. Section 1815(e). The cross-guarantee provision imposes liability on an insured depository institution for losses incurred by the FDIC in connection with the default of, or assistance provided to, a commonly controlled insured depository institution.

36. The 59 subsidiaries at the time of Mr. Abboud's takeover in 1988 had been reduced to 20.

37. Grant, p. 247.

38. "Texas Bank Firm And FDIC Agree on Initial Payment," *The Wall Street Journal*, January 19, 1994, p. A4.

39. Seidman, pp. 157–158.

40. Ibid., p. 157.

41. Grant, passim.

42. The TAB banks were closed prior to the existence of FIRREA and its cross-guarantee clause.

43. Federal Deposit Insurance Corporation, *History of the Eighties; Lessons for the Future*, 1997, Tables 1.1 and 1.2.

44. Ibid.

45. The insurance fund decline in 1947 was due to the repayment of capital stock subscribed by the Federal Reserve Banks and the U.S. Treasury when the FDIC was established, not to an operating loss.

46. Grant, p. 2.

47. Ibid., p. 94.

48. Ibid., p. 151.

49. Ibid., p. 168.

50. Ibid., p. 169.

51. Ibid., p. 249.

52. Ibid., p. 231.

53. Rank as of June 1989.

54. Grant, pp. 234–238.

55. "Northeast Officials Set to Monitor Regulators," *American Banker*, April 20, 1990, p. 1.

56. Grant, p. 238.

57. Seidman, p. 158.

6

FIRREA, and the FDIC as Top Dog

Notwithstanding the Texas problems, L. William Seidman and the FDIC were still sitting pretty in 1989. The savings and loan crisis had finally penetrated the nation's, and Congress's, consciousness, the federal thrift regulatory apparatus—the Federal Home Loan Bank Board and the Federal Savings and Loan Insurance Corporation—were in disrepute, and the FDIC seemed a likely rescuer. No shrinking violet, Chairman Seidman was an Old Washington Hand and well-respected on Capitol Hill. He skillfully moved the FDIC to the forefront of the effort to clean up the S&L debacle.

And a debacle it was. The FSLIC had a balance of $4.6 billion at year-end 1985 and was essentially insolvent at year-end 1986.[1] Despite reputable studies estimating substantial future losses from failed S&Ls—for example, $16 billion by the FHLBB staff in 1985, $20 billion by the General Accounting Office and $24 billion by FHLBB Chairman Edwin Gray in 1986—Congress made only a feeble rescue attempt in the Competitive Equality Banking Act of 1987 (CEBA). The law authorized $10.825 billion for recapitalization of the FSLIC, an amount widely viewed even as CEBA was passed as inadequate. A major reason Congress did not come to grips with the problem was the opposition of the S&L industry itself, a number of whose members apparently believed that more funding would result in the closing of viable institutions by the FSLIC and the FHLBB. The attitude seemed to be that if only the feds would keep their hands off, the industry could grow out of its problems. Moreover, although Texas politicians had not and were not to come to bat for the state's banks, at least one, House Majority Leader and later Speaker Jim Wright, for a time did the bidding of the state's S&Ls, which accounted for a hefty proportion of the national S&L problem. Mr. Wright was a factor in Congress's failure in 1986–87 to institute a meaningful federal attack on the exploding S&L disaster.[2]

Although its inadequate crack at handling the S&L crisis was largely mooted by the passage two years later of the Financial Institutions Reform, Recovery, and

Enforcement Act (FIRREA), CEBA did contain one provision that had a long term impact on the effort.[3] The manner in which Congress provided the funds to recapitalize the FSLIC both served as a model for the portion of FIRREA designed to pay for the S&L cleanup and was to cause a headache for legislators, regulators, and the banking and thrift industries in the middle of the next decade. The manner of providing funds was also symbolic of the reluctance of elected officials for much of the 1980s to confront the problems of the bank and thrift industries directly. If the problems could be approached obliquely, so much the better. In CEBA, Congress and the Reagan administration eschewed directly appropriating funds to recapitalize the FSLIC. Instead, they took a page from the creative financing manuals of the merger and acquisition specialists who were stars of the business world in the mid– and late–1980s. Business schools were the rage, MBAs were in their glory, and creative financing was approaching an art form. And creative financing provided a way to keep costs off the federal budget, the federal budget deficit being a perennial issue, and a matter of much political anguish, in the last several decades of the twentieth century.

CEBA created the Financing Corporation (FICO). With approximately $3.0 billion in capital from the Federal Home Loan Banks, the FICO purchased zero-coupon U.S. Treasury securities. These securities served as collateral for the issuance of 30-year interest-bearing debt obligations by the FICO. The proceeds from these obligations were channeled by the FICO to the FSLIC. From 1987 to 1989, the FICO issued approximately $8.2 billion in bonds. At maturity, the principal value of the bonds will be paid with the proceeds of the simultaneously maturing zero-coupon Treasury securities. By funneling the funds to recapitalize the FSLIC through the mechanism of a funding corporation, Congress avoided an increase in the federal debt that could be attributable directly to an S&L bailout. As part of its fiscal operations, the federal government is continually paying off maturing debt obligations and selling new obligations. If some of those new obligations happen to be purchased by a government-created entity that in effect uses them as collateral for its own borrowing, who can quantify a definitive increase in the federal debt? Certainly not the politicians who approve such off-budget creativity. Of course, a cynic might call this a form of money laundering: the relationship between the source and use of funds is obscured, giving the use a veneer that blurs the fiscal involvement and responsibility of the federal government. Opponents contended that the funding mechanism was a charade, and were to do so again when a similar scheme was proposed two years later in the development of FIRREA.

To jump ahead chronologically, the trouble that this arrangement caused in the mid–1990s concerned the interest payments on the FICO bonds. The principal repayment was to come from the Treasury zero-coupon bonds, but the annual interest expense was an industry responsibility, and the industry was shrinking. In CEBA, Congress made FSLIC-insured institutions responsible for the interest payments. When FSLIC was abolished in FIRREA in 1989 and replaced with the Savings Association Insurance Fund (SAIF)-insured institutions assumed the interest responsibility, which amounted to approximately $793 million a year. The money came from deposit insurance assessments paid by the SAIF-insured institutions. The assessments, however, were also the source of funds to capitalize the SAIF, the target capitalization level, established in FIRREA, being 1.25 percent of insured deposits. FIRREA also established a target capitalization of 1.25 percent of insured deposits for the Bank Insurance Fund (BIF).

After surviving the travails described in the next chapters, the banking industry, aided by a lengthy period of economic prosperity, not only recovered but soared to new heights of earnings and profitability.[4] The BIF, no longer being drained by bank failures, reached its required capitalization level in the second quarter of 1995. The FDIC, as required by law, lowered the deposit insurance assessments for BIF-insured institutions. The average BIF assessment rate went from 23.3 cents per $100 of assessable deposits to just 0.4 cents.[5] Because, however, at 0.47 percent of insured deposits in the fourth quarter of 1995 the SAIF was far from its required capitalization level, SAIF assessments could not be reduced. The average assessment rate for SAIF members remained at 23.7 cents per $100 of assessable deposits. Due in large measure to the diversion of a portion of SAIF assessments to the interest payments on the FICO bonds, the SAIF was years away from achieving the required capitalization level. Even when the 1.25 percent target was reached, sufficient assessments would have to be collected to meet the FICO interest payments. Consequently, the disparity between BIF and SAIF assessment rates was expected to exist for some time.

Fearing the disparity would cause an exodus from the SAIF—an exodus that indeed was beginning and that could eventually result in the FICO not receiving from SAIF-insured institutions sufficient assessment revenue to meet the interest on the FICO bonds—Congress, prodded by the banking regulators, took action. In the Deposit Insurance Funds Act of 1996, SAIF-insured institutions were subjected to a one-time assessment to raise the SAIF capitalization level to the required 1.25 percent of insured deposits. And responsibility for the FICO interest payments was expanded to include BIF-insured institutions. The effort to obviate the possibility of a default on the FICO interest payments took more than a year and a half of hard politicking. Ultimately, the effort was successful, but it was necessary only because nine years earlier Congress, with the encouragement and connivance of the Reagan administration, had opted for obliqueness over directness, financial "cuteness" over fiscal straightforwardness. Sometimes the chickens come home to roost.

But to return to larger events, by the end of 1988 the shortcomings of Congress's attempt in CEBA to cap the S&L crisis and the imperative for a large-scale federal effort were apparent to all but the most obtuse. The FSLIC was generally acknowledged to be deep in the red, and indeed would report a year-end deficit of $75 billion.[6] The congressional elections of the year were over, so the political incentive to delay facing a problem for which both parties could be blamed had abated. And the FHLBB under Mr. Gray's successor, Danny Wall, finished the year with a flurry of very public transactions in which investors acquired failing S&Ls on what many observers perceived as extremely favorable terms for the investors, and extremely unfavorable terms for the government. Spurred by tax breaks that were expiring on December 31, the transactions were part of the so-called Southwest Plan, which was designed to resolve insolvencies quickly while conserving the FSLIC's precious, limited cash. Failing institutions were grouped and marketed as a package, and acquirers were tempted with tax savings and various types of FSLIC notes and guarantees.[7]

Although perhaps admirable as a well-meaning effort to resolve the S&Ls industry's problems with the inadequate resources given by Congress, the year-end transactions and the Southwest Plan turned out to be professional disasters for Danny Wall. The perception that his relatively inexperienced staff of government bureaucrats had been taken advantage of by Wall Street sharpies and their clients in the hinterlands led Mr. Wall to be heaped with way more responsibility for the S&L crisis than he deserved. Mr. Wall just happened to be around for the end. The seeds have been sown, the plants had grown, and the fruits had ripened and begun rotting and falling long before he assumed a position of responsibility.[8]

FIRREA —CHRONOLOGY AND ISSUES

The Financial Institutions Reform, Recovery, and Enforcement Act, the law that finally recognized and tackled the S&L crisis in a meaningful manner, was signed by President George Bush on August 9, 1989. The milestones of FIRREA's passage were:

- On February 6, 1989, President Bush outlined a broad plan to address the S&L crisis.
- On February 7, pursuant to a management agreement between the FHLBB, the FSLIC, and the FDIC and as part of the administration's plan, the FDIC in effect assumed control of 222 insolvent thrifts.
- The administration's plan was introduced in the Senate on February 22 and in the House of Representatives on March 6.
- On April 19, the Senate passed its version. The House bill was passed on June 15.
- The House-Senate conference committee to iron out the differences between the two versions first reported out a bill on July 27. The administration threatened a veto because of disagreement over whether the funding was to be on or off budget. A compromise was reached and passed by both houses of Congress on August 4.
- The bill, H.R. 1278, was signed by the president on August 9, becoming Public Law 101–73.

Around these milestones were numerous committee and subcommittee hearings, considerable posturing and maneuvering on the part of legislative and executive branch officials and private sector lobbyists, and much editorial commentary. Among the individuals who played prominent roles in the development and passage of FIRREA were House Banking Committee Chairman Henry Gonzalez, Senate Banking Committee Chairman Donald Riegle, Treasury Secretary Nicholas Brady, Treasury Deputy Secretary John Robson, White House assistant Richard Breeden, Office of Management and Budget Director Richard Darman, and FDIC Chairman William Seidman.

In January 1989, the "reverse toaster" controversy presaged the difficulty and contentiousness of FIRREA's development over the months ahead. Reports surfaced that one possible element of the deposit insurance reform program being put together by the Bush administration was a fee on bank deposits, the fee proceeds to go to the deposit insurance fund. The reaction in Congress, from the banking industry, and on the editorial pages was quick and almost universally negative. Ever quick with a quip, Mr. Seidman captured the tone of the moment, and created some hard feelings on the part of a few within the administration, by characterizing the fee as a "reverse toaster," the reference being to the small appliances and other gifts that banks often gave new depositors. The depositor fee idea had a rather short life.

The plan that the Bush administration advanced in February of 1989 had a number of elements. To deal with insolvent thrifts, a limited life organization, to be called the Resolution Trust Corporation, would be created. The RTC would be authorized $50 billion to do its work of closing down or otherwise disposing of insolvent S&Ls. Building upon CEBA precedent, the funding would be off-budget. A funding corporation, the Resolution Funding Corporation, would be authorized to issue $50 billion in 30-year bonds. To provide for repayment of the principal, $5 to $6 billion of long term zero-coupon Treasury obligations would be purchased with S&L industry funds—Federal Home Loan Bank retained earnings plus S&L assessment premiums. Annual interest on the bonds would be met by proceeds from the liquidation of insolvent S&L assets and by retained earnings of the Federal Home Loan Banks. Any shortfalls from these sources would come from the Treasury. These makeup interest payments from the Treasury would be the only on-budget U.S. government expenditures for the S&L industry cleanup.

To attack what was perceived as inadequate supervision and too much industry influence, substantial revisions would be made in the federal oversight scheme for S&Ls. The deposit insurance function of the Federal Savings and Loan Insurance Corporation (FSLIC) would be transferred to the FDIC, although the bank and S&L insurance funds would not be commingled. The Federal Home Loan Bank Board would be abolished, and the new S&L regulatory structure placed within the Treasury Department, which had housed the national bank regulator, the Comptroller of the Currency, for over 100 years. These changes would result in the separation of the S&L chartering and deposit insurance functions, which would likely improve disciplinary standards through a system of supervisory checks and balances for S&Ls that closely paralleled the seemingly more successful system for commercial banks.

Both banks and thrifts would be subject to higher deposit insurance premiums. For banks, the purpose was to replenish the depleted bank insurance fund, which due in large measure to the Texas situation was known to have fallen in 1988—the actual results were not in when the plan was announced in early 1989—from the year-end 1987 balance of $18.3 billion, the pre-1990s apogee. The purpose for thrifts was to recapitalize the empty thrift insurance fund. Bank premiums would increase from 0.083 percent of deposits to 0.12 percent in 1990 and 0.15 percent thereafter. Thrift premiums would increase from 0.208 percent of deposits in 1990 to 0.23 percent for 1991 through 1993, declining to 0.18 percent in 1994. The explicit goal for both the bank and thrift insurance funds was to be a balance equal to 1.25 percent of insured deposits, which would be the first explicit statutory goal for the deposit insurance funds in the history of federal deposit insurance.

The administration plan would also phase in capital standards for thrifts that would be no less stringent than the standards for national banks, enhance the enforcement powers of the regulatory agencies, and increase the potential penalties for violations of statutes and regulations.

Much of the administration's plan found its way into the final bill. The legislative process was far from smooth, however, and the fleshing out of the details involved considerable give and take and the resolution of a number of difficult issues. The major topics that were the subject of dispute at one time or another between the unveiling of the plan in February 1989 and the enactment of FIRREA in August were: deposit insurance premiums; a thrift deposit insurance logo; thrift capital requirements; management and oversight of the RTC; and whether funding was to be on or off budget.

Deposit Insurance Premiums

The proposal to raise deposit insurance premiums for both banks and thrifts quite naturally encountered opposition. One frequent criticism during the debate was that the bank and thrift industries would be hit with higher costs—the increased premiums—just at a time when their profitability was being sorely tested. The industries found very little sympathy, however. Congress and the public were not inclined to be kind toward those who were now perceived as the cause of so much distress and aggravation.

Even though the administration called for separate bank and thrift deposit insurance funds and the maintenance of distinct regulatory structures for the two industries, the banking industry harbored a deep suspicion that it would be presented with the bill for at least a portion of the S&L cleanup. Specifically, banks vehemently reacted to any hint that bank insurance premiums would be used to rebuild the thrift insurance fund. During the months of debate on FIRREA's development, the banking industry expended much energy countering the possibility that it would be saddled with any of the cost of thrift failures. The banks were successful in 1989, but events seven years in the future when, in the Deposit Insurance Funds Act of 1996, banks were given a share of the responsibility for the FICO interest payments show that their fears were not groundless. Which, parenthetically, is not to say that banks were without some ill-defined degree of responsibility for the S&Ls' problems. Banks and thrifts were both members of an industry, the depository institutions industry, that was burdened with excess capacity and an antiquated structure. The structure and other conditions that produced the excess capacity were the result in part of industry efforts over many decades to avoid or mitigate the rigors of the marketplace. Thus suggesting that all sectors of the depository institutions industry should participate in its rehabilitation had a certain cosmic logic.

The FIRREA raised deposit insurance premiums pretty much in accordance with the administration's proposal. Minimum premiums for the thrift insurance fund, henceforth to be known as the SAIF, were to go from 0.208 percent of deposits to 0.23 percent in 1993. They would fall back to 0.18 percent in 1994 and 0.15 percent in 1998. Minimum premiums for the bank fund, henceforth to be known as the BIF, would jump to 0.12 percent in 1990 and 0.15 percent in 1991. Under certain specified conditions, the FDIC could impose rates above the minimums, but in no event higher than 0.325 percent. An explicit reserves-to-insured-deposits goal of 1.25 percent was specified for both funds. For the BIF, Congress's wording seemed to suggest that the goal be achieved by 1995.

Deposit Insurance Logo

The banking industry probably expended an equal amount of energy on what in hindsight seems a fairly minor issue. Since the thrift insurance fund was now to be under the care of the FDIC, a logical assumption was that thrifts should be able to display the FDIC sticker, just as banks had long done. Many in the banking industry, however, reacted to this idea as if they had been asked to share their spouses, and for far less than the $100,000 deposit insurance limit.

Bankers had a proprietary attitude toward the FDIC and, if truth be told, a certain smugness concerning the thrift industry and its problems. Allowing thrifts to display the FDIC logo, even though they were to be insured by the FDIC, struck many bankers as being a little too generous. Thrifts were not banks, and any actions or symbols implying that they might be on the same footing as banks were to be resisted.

The administration's plan was a bit vague as to the logo issue, stating merely, "Logos, properly representing the facts, to be determined." Informally, however, the possibility that thrifts might be allowed to sport FDIC stickers was advanced. The negative reaction of elements of the banking industry was so strong as to threaten generally favorable industry support for the plan as a whole. Consequently, FIRREA mandated a logo for SAIF-insured thrifts that was to be unmistakably different from the simple FDIC sticker displayed by banks.

Thrift Capital Requirements

A dispute having more concrete consequences involved the administration's proposal to have thrifts meet the capital requirements applicable to national banks by June 1, 1991. This would amount to an almost doubling of the then applicable thrift capital standards. It would also mean the end to the FHLBB practice of allowing thrifts to count balance sheet goodwill, which comes into being in merger and acquisition transactions, as capital. The proposal was attacked generally by many in the thrift industry as being too stringent. It was also attacked as being unfair to those who had acquired failed and failing thrifts with help from the FHLBB in the form of the treatment of goodwill as capital. By effectively nullifying the goodwill-as-capital provisions of these transactions, the administration's proposal would imperil the solvency of many of the acquired institutions.

Debate on the thrift capital issue continued throughout the legislative process. The potential impact of redefining thrift capital to exclude goodwill was perhaps the most contentious aspect of the debate. A number of members of Congress and other observers predicted years of litigation and a large bill in damages for breaches of contract if the FHLBB-blessed treatment of goodwill in the many ailing thrift acquisitions of the previous few years was negated. Consideration of the capital issue in the House became exceedingly complex, with the fight being waged not only substantively in the Banking Committee but also, in the latter stages, through intricate parliamentary maneuverings in the Rules Committee.[9]

For many thrifts, the outcome of the debates over capital would mean the difference between failure and continued existence. More generally, the outcome was awaited as an indicator of whether the industry still possessed, in spite of the problems of recent years, its historically strong influence in the halls of Congress. A headline in the *American Banker* the day after the House vote on June 18 provided an answer, and told of a new reality: "Options Dwindling for Stunned S&L Lobby; Capitol Hill's 'Get Tough' Mood Is Seen in Lopsided House Vote." The once powerful thrift lobby could no longer deliver. As recently as 24 months earlier, in the ineffective CEBA, that lobby had been able to head off any serious action regarding the developing crisis. But the enormity of the problems, and the resulting increased level of public scrutiny, had at last rendered the thrift industry politically impotent.

The final bill that became FIRREA mandated three separate capital standards for thrifts. All three standards were subject to the general admonition that they be "no less stringent" than the capital standards applicable to national banks. The first standard was a leverage limit of not less than 3 percent, calculated as the ratio of core capital to total assets. Initially, one-half of the core capital could be supervisory goodwill, but the inclusion of goodwill had to be phased out by 1995. The second standard was a tangible capital requirement of not less than 1.5 percent of total assets. The third standard was a risk-based capital requirement similar to the risk-based capital requirement applicable to national banks. The new thrift regulator, the Office of Thrift Supervision (OTS), was to promulgate regulations implementing the capital standards.

Concerning the negation of the favorable treatment by the FHLBB of goodwill in acquisitions of ailing thrifts, the critics proved to be correct. Years of litigation ensued. At first, the government largely prevailed. But in 1996, the U.S. Supreme Court ruled in *U.S. v. Winstar Corporation*[10] that the affected financial institutions had causes of action. The Court held that the government breached contracts to permit financial institutions to use special accounting methods in the acquisitions of failing thrifts when its regulatory agencies, pursuant to FIRREA, barred the use of the methods. Thus FIRREA's attempted negation of the FHLBB treatment of the goodwill generated in the acquisitions of failing institutions joined CEBA's scheme for the FICO interest payments as ill-advised congressional efforts to avoid the fiscal realities attending the S&L crisis.

RTC Management and Oversight

Probably the most distinctive feature of the Administration's proposal was how the several hundred dead and dying thrifts were to be handled. In the words of the White House fact sheet summarizing the proposal: "The President's plan will create a new Resolution Trust Corp. to resolve currently insolvent S&Ls in an orderly fashion. The creation of this *private* corporation is proposed for practical business reasons. It will allow isolation of insolvent S&Ls during the resolution process, and it will facilitate a full and precise accounting of all funds that are needed. (Emphasis added.)"[11]

Initially, the concept of a new, specially created entity to deal with the moribund portion of the thrift industry was just that, a concept. That not a lot of thinking had yet been devoted to the matter was evident a week later when the White House released a detailed summary of the proposed legislation.[12] The notion of a *private* corporation was nowhere to be found. Instead, the RTC was to be "created and managed by the FDIC." The deposit insurer was by no means to have a free hand, however. The work and progress of the RTC were to be subject to review by an RTC oversight board, which was to be comprised of the secretary of the treasury as chairman, the chairman of the Federal Reserve Board, and the comptroller general of the United States. The division of responsibility between the FDIC and the oversight board was far from clear. Confusion about the FDIC's role was further clouded by a statement in the legislation summary that the RTC would contract with the FDIC and private sources to provide management of the institutions conveyed to the RTC. Thus the FDIC would not only create and manage the RTC but would also work for it as a contractor.

Although other issues concerning the administration's plan often occupied the media's attention during the first few months of the legislative process, within the government the issues of the management and oversight of the RTC rarely left the foreground. And as other matters were resolved, public attention began shifting to the differing views about the structure of the new entity. Heightening media interest was the fact that the feisty, entertaining, quotable chairman of the FDIC seemed to be at odds with the administration.

As he described in his book on his government years, L. William Seidman was indeed in disagreement with how the administration wanted to proceed.[13] The basic positions were readily understandable. The administration and others saw the FDIC as being the major source of government expertise regarding the closing of depository institutions and the disposition of their assets, and therefore wanted the agency involved at the operating level. The administration, however, wanted to maintain control over the highly visible, politically charged expenditure of the huge amount of funds that would be involved in the S&L cleanup. For its part, the FDIC wanted, if it was to be involved in the S&L cleanup, as free a hand as possible in bringing its expertise to bear.

Another factor complicated these naturally opposing stances. The FDIC cherished its status as an independent agency, particularly one that, being financed by insurance assessments on the regulated industry, was supposedly not dependent on taxpayer funds.[14] The FDIC viewed having to answer to an administration-controlled oversight board as conflicting with its independence. That very independence, however, apparently made many in the administration wary of giving the FDIC too much leeway. Perhaps if the FDIC had been a little more discreet and tactful in exercising its independence, the degree of wariness would have been less. But under Chairman Seidman, the agency had not been bashful in touting its separate and distinct existence. Moreover, because of his outspokenness,

Chairman Seidman was apparently not viewed by some administrative officials as a total team player. His "reverse toaster" remark in January was just one example of the type of thing that most likely grated on White House and Treasury Department nerves.

Such personal and bureaucratic considerations may have exacerbated the situation, but at heart there was indeed a new question of governmental functions and structure. The FDIC had expertise regarding the closing of failed institutions and the disposition of their assets. But in the past, the FDIC had only worked with monies from the industry-built deposit insurance fund. The monies to resolve the S&L crisis were to be appropriated by Congress. Many believed that if it were given a taxpayer-financed role in the S&L crisis, the FDIC should be subject to greater oversight than it enjoyed regarding its private sector-financed activities.

The struggle over the RTC's structure, management, and oversight broke down into several subissues: the powers of the RTC oversight board versus the powers of RTC itself; the makeup of the RTC oversight board, including the matter of whether the FDIC was to have a seat on that board; and the role of the FDIC. Regarding the oversight board, the FDIC and its chairman felt strongly that if the FDIC was to be the operator of the RTC, the FDIC needed to be represented. The administration, on the other hand, argued that a board designed to review the work of the FDIC as operator of the RTC should not include the FDIC. One Treasury Department document stated: "It would be awkward and difficult for the oversight board to effectively oversee and evaluate the FDIC's managerial stewardship of the RTC if the FDIC held board membership."[15]

In late July, at the eleventh hour, a compromise between the administration and the FDIC was finally reached. Chairman Seidman described it thusly: "While strange compromises are not unusual in government, we ended up with an all-time classic."[16] In setting forth in great detail the rights and duties of the parties, the legislation resembled as much a contract or a treaty as it did a law. Operationally, the main entities enumerated in FIRREA to resolve the S&L crisis were the RTC, the FDIC, and the RTC Oversight Board. The FDIC was to be in effect the operating manager of the RTC. In fact, the RTC chairman and board were to be identical to the FDIC chairman and board. The purpose of the RTC was to "manage and resolve all cases" of thrifts failing between January 1, 1989, and August 7, 1992, subject to a number of guidelines. The RTC Oversight Board was to "oversee" the RTC, a function that included the development of strategies, policies, and goals, and the review of performance. Although the FDIC did not win representation on the RTC Oversight Board, the latter was required to perform much of its work "in consultation with" the RTC itself, whose management was of course the FDIC. The RTC Oversight Board was to consist of five members: the secretary of the treasury as chairman; the chairman of the Federal Reserve System; the secretary of Housing and Urban Development; and two independent persons selected by the president and confirmed by the Senate. Later in this chapter, the operational duties of the three entities, and the functions of the funding entities of the S&L cleanup, are described in greater detail.

On-Budget Versus Off-Budget

The final major matter of dispute in the development of FIRREA was whether the amount provided to deal with the failed S&Ls would appear in the budget of the U.S. government. This issue had also been a dominant factor two years earlier in the debates leading to the enactment of CEBA. Indeed, until the surprising appearance of a surplus in 1998, the federal budget deficit—the excess of expenditures over revenues—was a leading political issue of the 1980s and 1990s. Any proposal, however laudable or necessary its goal, to increase expenditures by the U.S. government ran a gauntlet of budget-guardians, which was not necessarily a bad thing. But creative minds often took the debates a step further and toyed with ways to "cook the books." The temptation to use alternatives other than direct, outright federal appropriations, and consequently to keep the expenditures from having a measurable accounting impact, was, and is, great.

If included in the federal budget, the $50 billion proposed for the S&L cleanup would be a real deficit-increaser. Neither political party wanted to be tagged with the responsibility of increasing the deficit, but because they occupied the White House, the Republicans were a bit more vulnerable. They could be more easily saddled with the moniker of financial irresponsibility. Consequently, the administration and Republican members of Congress were strongly in favor of an off-budget financing alternative.

The off-budget alternative was a funding corporation, similar to CEBA's FICO, that would issue long term debt instruments in the amount of $50 billion. The proceeds would be passed to the RTC. Interest on the bonds would be largely provided by the S&L industry through earnings of the Federal Home Loan Banks. To repay the $50 billion in approximately 30 years, $5 to $6 billion in zero-coupon U.S. Treasury bonds would be purchased with funds from the Federal Home Loan Banks. The arrangement would result in the outlays by the RTC to resolve failed S&Ls being "off" the federal budget. That is, the outlays would not legally be considered outlays by the U.S. government and would not be reflected in the government's budget. In addition, an exception to the Gramm-Rudman Act would not have to be made. That act set limits on federal government expenditures in relation to revenues, with the goal of eventually reaching a state of equality between the two.

Critics attacked the administration's proposal primarily on two grounds. First, the funding corporation bonds would likely carry a higher interest expense than would U.S. Treasury debt. Common estimates of the increased cost ranged from $125 million to $300 million a year, and from $4.5 billion to $5.0 billion overall. Thus maintaining the Gramm-Rudman course toward a technically balanced budget by putting the S&L rescue off-budget would come at a price.

A second criticism of the funding corporation approach by some skeptics was that it was a fiction. The ultimate source of the rescue outlays was Treasury debt—the zero-coupon bonds that the funding corporation would purchase to pay off the principal of its own 30-year bonds. Thus, these critics viewed the funding corporation mechanism as merely a means to obscure the source of the S&L rescue funds and to affect the timing of the funds' recognition in the federal budget.

More than a little portion of the criticism of the funding corporation approach also stemmed from political motives. One of Candidate George Bush's most emphatic pledges during the 1988 presidential election had been, "No New Taxes." At least a few of his political opponents would welcome the opportunity to have him eat those words. One way of preparing the meal would be to place the S&L rescue on the budget. To prevent the increase in expenditures from increasing the deficit without cutting expenditures elsewhere in the budget, President George Bush might be forced to propose a tax increase.

The Senate bill adopted on April 19, 1989, provided for off-budget financing. The House bill adopted on June 15 put the S&L rescue on-budget. The House-Senate conference committee opted for the House on-budget approach in the bill reported out at the end of July. But the administration was adamant in its opposition to an immediate $50 billion increase in on-budget financing. President Bush even took the unusual step of sending Congress a letter containing an explicit threat to veto any bill providing for on-budget financing.[17] The Democratic majority did not have enough votes to override a presidential veto of the bill, and importantly, Congress's August recess was imminent.

So an eleventh-hour compromise was reached. In the words of the *American Banker* headline, "Late-Night Showdown Leads to S&L Deal."[18] Of the $50 billion authorized in FIRREA for the S&L cleanup, $20 billion would be on-budget in 1989. The remaining $30 billion was to be raised off-budget by the funding corporation, called the Resolution Funding Corporation.

Somewhat surprisingly, the amount itself for the S&L cleanup was not a big issue during the months of FIRREA's gestation. Differing estimates regarding the cleanup's cost had been argued about during the year or so preceding the first half of 1989, and shortly after FIRREA's enactment the total cost of the rescue again became a principal subject of debate. But during the period of February to August, 1989, comparatively little questioning of the $50 billion estimate occurred. Committing the government to the cleanup and hammering out the structural details temporarily relegated the question of cost to the back burner.

THE LAW

All of FIRREA's length and complexity were focused mainly on two items: the regulatory structure for the S&L industry and the cleanup of that industry. Concerning the former, the law made one of only a handful of significant changes in the regulatory structure for the banking and thrift industries since the establishment of the modern system during the 1930s. The independent FHLBB and its subsidiary insurer, the FSLIC, were abolished. Taking the FHLBB's place as the thrift regulator was the Office of Thrift Supervision, which joined the Office of the Comptroller of the Currency in the Treasury Department. The supervisory and regulatory system for national banks—situated in the Treasury Department—was deemed enough of a long term success by the administration and Congress to provide a model for the new system for thrifts. Events had shown that an independent regulator whose mandate included the promotion of the regulated industry was less than ideal. Taking the FHLBB's place as overseer of the Federal

Home Loan Bank System was a five-member Federal Housing Finance Board, the five members being the secretary of the Department of Housing and Urban Development and four other individuals appointed by the president and confirmed by the Senate. Deposit insurance responsibility for thrifts was given to the FDIC, which was to administer a separate thrift deposit insurance fund, the Savings Association Insurance Fund. The deposit insurance fund for banks was henceforth termed the Bank Insurance Fund.

The S&L industry cleanup was to be a complex affair. On the operating side were the Oversight Board, the Resolution Trust Corporation, and the FDIC. On the funding side were the Resolution Funding Corporation and the FSLIC Resolution Fund. CEBA's FICO remained in existence, although it did not issue any further obligations and consequently did not provide any further funds for the cleanup.[19]

On the Oversight Board were the secretary of the Treasury, who would serve as chairman, the secretary of Housing and Urban Development, the chairman of the Federal Reserve System, and two independent persons chosen by the president and confirmed by the Senate. The Oversight Board's purpose was to review and have overall responsibility for the RTC's activities. The board, however, would not be involved in or responsible for individual institutions or cases, specific asset dispositions, or in general the day-to-day operations of the RTC. Specific duties of the Oversight Board included establishing strategic plans and overall goals for the RTC, approving periodic financing requests, reviewing the RTC's performance, establishing national and regional advisory boards, and approving all RTC rules, regulations, and guidelines. After consultation with the RTC, the board could require modification of these rules, regulations, and guidelines. An initial statutorily required task for the Oversight Board was to develop, in consultation with the RTC, a strategic plan. The plan was to be a detailed description of the RTC's goals and methods. Among the 17 items that the plan at a minimum was to include were: factors for selecting the order in which failed institutions or categories of institutions would be resolved; standards for selecting the appropriate resolution method; plans for the disposition of assets; and management objectives by which the RTC's progress could be measured.

The RTC was to be the hands-on operator for the S&L cleanup. It had three principal enumerated duties: (1) to resolve all cases of formerly FSLIC-insured institutions placed in conservatorship or receivership between January 1, 1989, and three years after the date of FIRREA's enactment, or August 9, 1992; (2) to liquidate the Federal Asset Disposition Association, an agency that had been chartered by the FHLBB in 1985 to manage and dispose of the assets of failed thrifts; and (3) to conduct its operations so as to maximize recovery on the assets it was to acquire, minimize the impact of its activities on local markets, make efficient use of its funds, minimize losses incurred in resolving cases, and maximize preservation of affordable housing. Unless removed by the Oversight Board, the FDIC was to be the exclusive manager of the RTC, and the RTC was to have no employees of its own. The Board of Directors of the FDIC was to be the Board of Directors of the RTC, the chairman of the FDIC was to be the chairman of the RTC, and the RTC was to be staffed by personnel detailed from the FDIC and other federal agencies. The Oversight Board could remove the FDIC as exclusive manager of the RTC, but only for certain extraordinary reasons enumerated in the statute.

In addition to the general mandates in the third category of duties, the RTC was subject to several other restrictions regarding how it was to conduct its activities. To the extent they were available and their use practicable and efficient, private sector sources were to be relied upon. Independent contractors, however, were to be subject to stringent ethical standards and conflict of interest regulations. Special asset-disposition procedures were to be formulated to protect the economies of distressed areas. And the disposition of single-family and multifamily residential properties was to be subject to detailed procedures designed to ensure that low- and moderate-income families received a portion of the sales.

The principal purpose of the Resolution Funding Corporation (REFCORP) was to raise the $30 billion in off-budget funds authorized by Congress, the remaining $20 billion of the $50 billion total being an on-budget appropriation. Essentially a conduit similar to CEBA's FICO, the REFCORP would use seed money, which eventually totaled $4.8 billion, from the Federal Home Loan Banks and the SAIF to purchase long term noninterest-bearing, or zero-coupon Treasury securities. The zero-couponTreasuries would back debt obligations—30–to 40–year bonds—issued by the REFCORP. The principal of the REFCORP bonds would be repaid with the proceeds of the simultaneously maturing zero-coupon Treasuries. Interest on the bonds would be met with proceeds from RTC liquidations of assets of failed thrifts and annual payments of up to $300 million from the Federal Home Loan Banks. In a wise departure from the FICO precedent, Congress provided that any shortfalls from these sources would be covered by transfers from the Treasury. Thus the danger of a crisis involving interest on REFCORP debt similar to the crisis involving interest on FICO debt described earlier in this chapter was not allowed to develop.

FIRREA also created another financial entity for the S&L cleanup, the FSLIC Resolution Fund (FRF). The primary purpose of the FRF, which was to be administered by the FDIC, was to liquidate the assets and contractual obligations of the now-defunct FSLIC. Those thrifts that failed before January 1, 1989, or that were assisted through August 8, 1989, were the FRF's responsibility. The FRF's backup funding source, after income from the management, and proceeds from the disposition, of the assets of failed institutions, was the U.S. Treasury.

In addition to its main focuses of restructuring the regulatory and supervisory system for the thrift industry and providing for the cleanup of that industry, FIRREA contained other provisions. Among them were the increases in deposit insurance premiums noted earlier. Although at the time of FIRREA's development and enactment the FDIC was generally viewed as the White Knight to the rescue, a wary eye was being cast on the insurance fund for banks. In April 1989, in the midst of the debate over the legislation that was shortly to become FIRREA, the FDIC announced the first operating loss in its history. As a result of the loss, the deposit insurance fund for banks declined from $18.3 billion at year-end 1987 to $14.1 billion at year-end 1988. Fears were increasing that the worst was yet to come. For banks, the statutorily mandated increase in deposit insurance premiums was for the purpose of rebuilding from incurred and expected losses.

FIRREA also included the cross-guarantee provision that the FDIC wanted as a result of its Texas experience. The provision would enable the FDIC, in the event of a failure of a bank or thrift, to collect damages from commonly controlled depository institutions.

EPILOGUE

Before returning in the next chapter to the banking crisis, which is about to explode in all its glory, the narrative should dispose of the S&L mess. Occasionally in the affairs of government, an entity unequivocally accomplishes its mission. Such was the case with the Resolution Trust Corporation. Under microscopic scrutiny, subject to carping and criticism of the first magnitude, the RTC plowed resolutely forward. Congress made changes in management, timing, and funding, but in the end the S&L industry was stripped of its dead and dying wood.

Managerially, the major change was the removal of the FDIC from the management of the RTC. In 1991, Congress replaced the Oversight Board with a less powerful and intrusive Thrift Depositor Protection Oversight Board, abolished the RTC Board of Directors, which had been the FDIC Board of Directors wearing a different hat, and replaced the FDIC as manager of the RTC with a chief executive officer of the RTC.[20] Concerning timing, FIRREA had given the RTC responsibility for resolving thrifts for which a receiver or conservator was appointed during the period January 1, 1989, through August 9, 1992. The period was eventually extended to June 30, 1995.[21] As for funding, Congress ultimately made a total of $105 billion available to the RTC to cover losses associated with the resolutions of failing and failed thrifts.[22] An estimated $17.1 billion of the total $105 billion will likely not be needed.[23]

All told, the RTC closed 747 institutions with assets at the time they entered the conservatorship phase of $402 billion. The RTC fulfilled the government's pledge to insured depositors by protecting 25 million depositor accounts. Of the $277 billion in liabilities at resolution, approximately $221 billion represented liabilities to depositors. The General Accounting Office has estimated the total noninterest cost of the S&L cleanup, including both the RTC phase and the pre-RTC phase when the FSLIC was responsible for the resolutions, to be $160.1 billion, of which $132.1 billion was provided from taxpayer funding sources. Interest costs were estimated at $209.0 billion.[24]

NOTES

1. National Commission on Financial Institution Reform, Recovery and Enforcement (hereinafter NCFIRRE), *Origins and Causes of the S&L Debacle: A Blueprint for Reform* (Washington, D.C., 1993), pp. 57–59.

2. See Ibid., p. 58.

3. CEBA also contained a "full faith and credit" provision: "It is the sense of the Congress that it should affirm that deposits up to the statutorily prescribed amount in federally insured depository institutions are backed by the full faith and credit of the United States" (Section 901). Some commentators have seen this explicit statement of government backing for

deposit insurance as significant. Others view it merely as an affirmation of a government guarantee that has been the foundation of federal deposit insurance since its inception.

4.   See Chapter 8. Earnings—net income—for U.S. commercial banks reached a record of $32.0 billion for 1992, and set a new record every year thereafter through 1997: $43.1 billion for 1993, $44.6 billion for 1994, $48.7 billion for 1995, $52.4 billion for 1996, and $59.2 billion for 1997. Profitability as measured by annual return on assets set a record of 1.23 percent in 1997.

5.   Federal Deposit Insurance Corporation, *Quarterly Bank Profile*, 4th Quarter 1995, p. 15.

6.   Federal Home Loan Bank Board, *Annual Report, 1988*, p. 36.

7.   See NCFIRRE, pp. 60-61.

8.   On the other hand, one should note that Mr. Wall was not a completely innocent victim. As staff director of the Senate Banking Committee from 1980 to 1986, he had a small hand in the ill-designed and poorly implemented deregulatory efforts that exacerbated the problems of the S&L industry as it attempted to cope with its long term structural deformities.

9.   For a review of the Rules Committee treatment of the thrift rescue legislation, see the *American Banker* issues of June 6, 7, 8, 9, 14, 15, and 16, 1989.

10.   116 S. Ct. 2432.

11.   Reprinted in the *American Banker*, February 8, 1989, p. 4.

12.   Reprinted in the *American Banker*, February 16, 1993, p. 4.

13.   L. William Seidman, *Full Faith and Credit* (New York: Times Books, 1993), pp. 198–204.

14.   Some observers argue that the FDIC's belief in its financial independence does not quite match the facts. These observers argue that the ultimate underpinning of financial stability in the United States is the full faith and credit of the federal government.   Only that underpinning enables the FDIC both to handle failed institutions and to finance its operations out of deposit insurance fund that is only a tiny fraction—it has never been higher than 2 percent—of insured deposits.

15.   Quoted in the *American Banker*, July 12, 1993, p. 22.

16.   Seidman, p. 202.

17.   "Bush Threatens Veto on S&L Bill in Budget Fight," *American Banker*, August 4, 1989; "Late-Night Showdown Leads to S&L Deal," *American Banker*, August 7, 1989.

18.   *American Banker*, August 7, 1989.

19.   FICO's borrowing authority was terminated in the Resolution Trust Corporation Refinancing, Restructuring and Improvement Act of 1991.

20.   Title III of the Resolution Trust Corporation Refinancing, Restructuring and Improvement Act of 1991.

21.   The period was extended to September 30, 1993, by the Resolution Trust Corporation Refinancing, Restructuring and Improvement Act of 1991. In December 1993, the period was again extended, by the Resolution Trust Corporation Completion Act, to a date not earlier than January 1, 1995, nor later than July 1, 1995. The final date of June 30, 1995, was selected by the chairperson of the Thrift Depositor Protection Oversight Board. FIRREA had provided that the RTC was to cease to exist on December 31, 1996. The Resolution Trust Corporation Completion Act of 1993 moved the termination date up to December 31, 1995.

22.   FIRREA provided $50 billion. The Resolution Trust Corporation Funding Act of 1991 provided an additional $30 billion. The Resolution Trust Corporation Refinancing, Restructuring and Improvement Act of 1991 provided $25 billion in December 1991, which was only available for obligation until April 1, 1992. In December 1993, the Resolution Trust Corporation Completion Act removed the April 1, 1992, deadline, thus making the balance of the $25 billion available.

23. General Accounting Office, *Financial Audit: Resolution Trust Corporation's 1995 and 1994 Financial Statements*, GAO/AIMID–96–123 (July 1996), p. 11.

24. Ibid., passim.

7

The Troubles Peak

The high point, or low point, of the banking troubles of the 1980s and early 1990s occurred during the two-year period between the enactment of FIRREA in August of 1989 and the enactment of FDICIA—the Federal Deposit Insurance Corporation Improvement Act—in December 1991. Although few realized it at the time of FDICIA's passage, the peak of the banking troubles was over, and the industry was on the road to recovery. That reality would not become apparent for some time, however. The belief that banks were in difficulty was to dominate public, congressional, policy-maker, and policy-kibitzer attitudes for several more years. Indeed, as chronicled in the next chapter, the condition of the banking industry became an issue late in the presidential campaign of 1992, courtesy of *The Washington Post* and Ross Perot.

In the public mind, the S&L crisis and the banking troubles were very much intertwined, even indistinguishable. This perception was not far from reality and might have worked to the benefit of the banking industry and its regulators. The attention accorded the RTC and its initial efforts deflected a goodly portion of the hysteria and hand-wringing that might have descended on the banking field. Bankers and their regulators certainly received attention, and were eventually burdened with an extreme piece of legislative micromanaging, FDICIA, but it could have been worse. An intriguing question for speculation is, if there had been no distracting S&L crisis, what additional public policy changes, over and above those actually made, would have been foisted on the banking field?

But the S&L crisis was the center of attention. Although Mr. Seidman had the RTC off to a fast start following the enactment of FIRREA in August 1989, second guessing of the cleanup agency's actions and decisions started almost immediately. The cumbersome management arrangement with the FDIC and the Oversight Board and the extensive controls and transparency that Congress built into the scheme invited a great amount of kibitzing from both inside and outside government. Far from being the czar of the S&L cleanup, Mr. Seidman was shortly in danger of being one of its victims. Moreover, many observers came to believe that Mr. Seidman and the FDIC could not deal with both the S&L crisis and the growing difficulties in the banking industry.

One problem, little commented on in the press, which tended to focus on the birth pangs of the RTC and the rocky relationship between Mr. Seidman and Treasury Department officials, was that much of the staffing for the new agency came from the FDIC. During the RTC's almost six and a half years of existence, approximately 2,000 FDIC employees worked at one time or another for the cleanup agency, most of them volunteering for the duty. RTC employment peaked at approximately 8,600 in April 1992.[1] Who were the FDIC staffers who volunteered for the RTC? A definitive analysis and survey was apparently never attempted, but one might make some conjectures. The RTC was portrayed in the media as facing a gargantuan task. Those in the bank regulatory agencies knew the portrayal was accurate. An individual going to the RTC could expect confusion, long hours, high levels of stress—and a challenge. Would the stereotype government bureaucrat forsake his or her familiar, comfortable, nine–to–five existence for such an environment? A speculation, and absent hard evidence it is only a speculation, is that the RTC attracted an inordinate proportion of the FDIC's "best and brightest." The irony is that the FDIC was about to have need for all the "best and brightest" it could find. The deposit insurer might have lost some of its most competent and energetic employees just when it required them the most.[2]

In addition to the S&L crisis, another event during the height of the banking difficulties diverted the attention of the public and the policy-makers. That event was a war, the Gulf War of 1990–91. Saddam Hussein invaded Kuwait in early August 1990, one year after passage of FIRREA. For the next nine months, and especially during the period late November 1990 through late March 1991, the S&L crisis, the banking crisis, economic conditions, and just about everything else played second fiddle to the war. Members of the media, even those specializing in subjects seemingly far removed from military matters, sought war angles for their efforts. Instead of piling on the S&L crisis, the banking troubles, or other attractions, the U.S. media piled on the U.S. military, first in derision at what was perceived as a clumsy, bumbling, technologically burdened giant who was going to get his clock cleaned, and then, at least for a few months, in unadulterated, effusive admiration for one of the most lopsided victories in the history of warfare. The U.S. banking industry might be in Saddam Hussein's debt for diverting attention during its blackest days since the Great Depression.

"WOES"

"Woes" was one of the favorite words of the *American Banker*'s headline writers from late 1989 through 1990:

Real Estate Woes Halt 3d Merger This Summer in New England—August 24, 1989;
Northeast Thrifts with Loan Woes Told to Cut Payments—August 28, 1989;

Junk Bond Woes Spark Fed to Reassure Stock Market That Large Banks Are Safe
—September 18, 1989;
Real Estate Woes Spur Big Loss at First Interstate's Arizona Unit—October 23,
1989;
Southeast Chief Sees Realty Woes as Pothole in the Road to a Boom—March 27,
1990;
Real Estate Woes Cut Net at C&S, Bank of Boston—April 27, 1990;
Realty Woes Depress Net at Citi, Chemical—July 18, 1990;
Woes Cutting Bank Capital as Tougher Rules Near—October 4, 1990;
Regulators, ABA Brass Confer on Image Woes—October 23, 1990.

Although they stretched across the country and involved a number of aspects of the banking business, the woes were concentrated in New England and real estate. The building glut that had begun in Texas had spread over the decade to other parts of the country, and the problems caused by the glut were now also spreading. New Englanders had embraced the real estate euphoria with particular enthusiasm; now they were being particularly hard-hit with the consequences.

In releasing data in December 1989 from bank filings for the third quarter of the year, the FDIC noted that real estate loans had grown from 25 percent of all commercial bank loans in 1983 to 35 percent in 1989.[3] Of the seven states whose banks had the highest concentration of real estate loans in their portfolios, four were in New England: real estate loans accounted for 60 percent of the portfolios of Vermont banks, 54 percent for Maine banks, 54 percent for Connecticut banks, and 48 percent for New Hampshire banks. Three New England states were among the 10 states with the highest ratio of noncurrent real estate loans to total real estate loans. Moreover, while most of the other seven states in this top 10 had shown improvement over previous reporting periods, the three New England states were heading in the opposite direction. The ratio of noncurrent real estate loans to total real estate loans was 4.76 percent for Massachusetts banks, 3.85 percent for Connecticut banks, and 3.69 percent for New Hampshire banks. In each instance, the ratio was more than three times the level of a year earlier. Year-end data released in March 1990 showed that the trend for New England banks was continuing. After just three short months, the ratio of noncurrent real estate loans to total real estate loans was up to 6.89 percent for Massachusetts banks, 6.12 percent for Connecticut banks, and 4.43 percent for New Hampshire banks.[4]

Real estate woes spawned or were part and parcel of other concerns of the banking industry, its regulators, and policy-makers in the several years following the passage of FIRREA. Foremost among these concerns were an alleged credit crunch, an alleged deterioration in the Bank Insurance Fund, and continuing bank failures. In 1991, the four topics became elements in the debate over banking reform legislation, a debate that resulted in December of that year in the enactment of FDICIA.

CREDIT CRUNCH

Cries about a credit crunch began soon after it became generally known that the regulators, particularly the Comptroller of the Currency, were shifting examiners to

New England. Potential borrowers in the region perceived a causal connection between the increased examination efforts and an increased difficulty in obtaining credit. The perception of tighter credit quickly spread to other areas of the nation. Naturally, politicians became involved, and from 1990 until well into 1993 charges and countercharges reverberated among frustrated borrowers, loan-shy bankers, defensive regulators, demanding legislators, compromising Bush and later Clinton administration officials, and pontificating academics.

Initially, Comptroller of the Currency Robert L. Clarke took the most heat. Two headlines in the *American Banker* tell the tale of the line he was having difficulty walking. An article on February 13, 1990, was introduced with, "Comptroller Warns Banks to Clean Up Realty Loans." The complaints were many and loud, and a headline two weeks later, on March 1, indicated a bit of back-stepping: "Comptroller Denies Intent to Halt Realty Loans." Congressman Joseph P. Kennedy helped arrange a meeting between bankers and regulators in April. In reporting the meeting, the *American Banker* pronounced: "The hottest topic in banking now is whether tight regulatory scrutiny on real estate portfolios is spurring a credit crunch."[5] Congressman Kennedy formed a committee with other politicians, including Massachusetts Governor Michael Dukakis, to monitor the "flow of credit" into New England.[6] In a hearing before the House of Representatives Small Business Committee, Congress Kennedy asserted that the "credit crunch is real."[7] In June, Congressman Kennedy took his complaints to a hearing before the Senate Banking Committee. The *American Banker* reported the hearing under the headline, "Regulators Get Lashing From Mass. Lawmakers."[8]

The Federal Reserve began to find evidence confirming, in its mind, if not a credit crunch, at least tighter credit.[9] The matter attracted attention at the highest level: in November 1990, President George Bush asked the regulators to explain what the heck was going on.[10] In early March 1991, the regulators, prodded by the Treasury Department, announced a plan to ease the credit crunch that now was generally conceded to exist.[11] The essence of the plan was to lighten up in the evaluation of real estate loans. An important component of the plan was explicitly informing bank examiners of the new leniency: plans can be ineffectual if the implementers aren't on board, and the distance between Washington and the troops in the field is often enormous. But expressions of dissatisfaction with bank examiners continued to come from high in the administration. A headline in September 1991 read, "Bush Says Examiners Still Impede Recovery."[12] Additional leniency measures were announced.[13] In December, Treasury Secretary Nicholas F. Brady let both examiners and the public know that the administration was still on the case: "Brady to Examiners: Use More Discretion."[14] Gradually the complaints and rhetoric eased, but as late as April 1993 the topic was still around. In an article entitled " 'Regulators from Hell' Frighten Some Banks But Also Win Praise," *The Wall Street Journal* asked whether tough bank examiners were just preventing another crisis, or were they causing a credit crunch?[15]

Had there in fact been a credit crunch? And if so, what caused it? Specifically, were the banking regulators responsible?

In the aftermath of the alleged credit crunch, the Federal Reserve Bank of New

York took an in-depth look at the evidence.[16] Overall, the bank's studies concluded that a credit crunch, or more properly a credit slowdown, did indeed occur.

For example, private nonfinancial debt grew 9.6 percent between 1960 and 1982 and 10.6 percent between 1982 and 1989, but only 3.1 percent during the period 1989–1992.[17] Moreover, the Northeast—New England and the Mid-Atlantic—and the Pacific regions experienced outright declines in total and business bank loans, thus validating the anguish of the New Englanders.[18]

But the causes of the credit slowdown were diffuse and not easy to isolate. On the demand side, the nation experienced a recession from July 1990 to March 1991. Less credit is demanded in an economic downturn than in a period of growth. Contributing to the anemic performance of the economy, and thus to reduced demand for credit, were the defense build-down and lower defense spending; corporate downsizing; historically low levels of consumer confidence; the overbuilt state of commercial real estate; and the overextended financial positions of households, businesses, and financial institutions. Demand for credit was also reduced by a widespread structural change taking place regarding inventories. Just-in-time inventory control and other management techniques were reducing the inventories maintained by businesses, especially in the manufacturing sector, and consequently the associated financing requirements.

On the supply side, both bank and nonbank creditors had appeared to tighten credit standards, thereby reducing the supply of credit. A principal motivation for the tightening on the part of banks was concern about their own weakening capital positions, which in turn reflected deteriorating loan quality and rising charge-offs. Among nonbank creditors, retrenchment by finance companies and life insurance companies was similarly due in part to worries about their own financial conditions, which were receiving critical scrutiny from credit rating agencies and state regulatory bodies. In the commercial paper market, numerous credit rating downgrades and an extraordinary number of defaults—15 since 1989 compared to only 2 in the market's entire previous history—hindered expansion to fill the void created by the pull-backs of banks, finance companies, life insurance companies, and others. The concerns of bank and nonbank creditors about their own financial condition were amplified when they considered the situations of their customers. The debt overhang that was causing many borrowers to forego further trips to the money well was finally registering on the suppliers of the well.

Given the interrelationships among the supply and demand factors causing the credit slowdown, could it be said the chain of causation began with the reduced supply of credit, which produced the recession, which in turn produced the fall in demand for credit? Starting from an even earlier step, did the chain begin with bank regulators who forced banks to tighten up their credit standards, which then led to the reduced supply of credit, the recession, and the fall in credit demand? That was certainly the belief of some. A rather bizarre argument along these lines was advanced by no less an authority than the deputy chief economist for the Securities and Exchange Commission, David S. Bizer. In an article in *The Wall Street Journal*, he contended that new capital standards and increased vigor on the part of bank examiners cost U.S. business and consumers $81 billion in unmade loans between 1989 and June 1992.[19] He implied that these unmade loans exacerbated the recession of 1990–91.

Difficulties with causation troubled even the nation's top economic guru, Federal Reserve Board Chairman Alan Greenspan. Testifying before the Senate Banking Committee in February 1991, he stated that overzealous regulation was one of the causes of the credit crunch. Barely two months later, however, bankers were at fault: he was chiding them for not lending more.[20] Other commentators were more circumspect than Messrs. Bizer and Greenspan. The studies of the New York Fed, for example, although attributing some responsibility for the credit slowdown to tighter capital requirements and more intensive supervisory oversight, concluded that such factors were very much overshadowed by market forces. Given the complexities and intricacies of economic activity, this conclusion seems more persuasive than the one-factor approach expounded by Bizer, notwithstanding the elegance and robustness of his quantitative methods.

The credit crunch controversy is another example of the human tendency and desire to simplify complex economic problems. The public, the media, and legislators like simple stories, preferably with easily identifiable villains. The economic problems that came to a head in the early 1990s were not simple. The causes and roots were many and interrelated, ranging from the debt overhang of the 1980s, to overbuilt real estate markets, to a restructuring of the depository institutions industry, to a defense build-down, to a delayed turn in the business cycle. But bankers and their regulators presented handy targets for the public's frustration, and accordingly were roundly excoriated. Maybe through such thrashings bankers and their regulators provide a psychic safety value for their fellow citizens.

AND YOU THOUGHT WEATHER FORECASTS CHANGED . . .

L. William Seidman left the FDIC in the fall of 1991 with his reputation for competence and foresight largely intact. One of the few blemishes on that reputation arose from his association with deteriorating statistics and forecasts regarding the condition of the FDIC's Bank Insurance Fund. From mid–1990 into 1992, the news about the BIF grew progressively worse, and as the man in charge for much of that period, Mr. Seidman's luster picked up a bit of tarnish.

Predictions of troubles in the banking industry and with the insurance fund for banks had been increasing for some time, but in 1990 policy-makers and the public began paying serious attention. One of the first warnings of dire times made during that year came from the respected Lowell L. Bryan of McKinsey & Co. In testimony in May before the Senate Banking Committee, he stated that a recession would wipe out the capital of 20 percent of the nation's commercial banks.[21] Fortunately, a recession was not expected: the *American Banker* article reporting Mr. Bryan's testimony also noted that four of the five members of a panel of the National Association of Business Economists believed no recession would occur through 1991. Unfortunately, the fifth member of the panel turned out to be correct: a recession began in July 1990 and lasted through March 1991. Fortunately, Mr. Bryan's prognostication that the capital of 20 percent of the nation's banks would be erased proved to be inaccurate.

The same day that Mr. Bryan testified, the FDIC announced the 1989 status of the BIF.[22] The fund lost $851 million for the year, standing at $13.2 billion at year-end. This was the second consecutive annual loss but better than the previous year's decline of $4.2 billion. More striking than the 1989 loss was the drop in coverage. The fund now had only 70 cents for every $100 of insured deposits, down from 80 cents at year-end 1988 and $1.19 at year-end 1985.

In July 1990, forecasts of decline began in earnest. Mr. Seidman indicated that the BIF could fall by as much as $2 billion for the year. He revised the projected loss to $3 billion in September and to $4 billion in December.[23] But he was operating in the low end of the range of forecasts. Pushing the outside of the envelop so to speak were two veterans of the thrift industry's decline and a think tank thinker. The thrift veterans were R. Dan Brumbaugh and James Barth. They had been among the first to predict the collapse of the S&L industry. The think tanker was Robert Litan, a long-time staffer of the Brookings Institution and a prolific author on matters concerning the financial industry.

Messrs. Brumbaugh, Barth, and Litan had been hired by a subcommittee of the House Banking Committee to analyze the health of the FDIC. Their report was months from completion and release, but Mr. Brumbaugh had already formed his opinion. In early July 1990 in an article headlined "Economist Says 'Insolvent' FDIC Is Covering Up," the *American Banker* quoted Mr. Brumbaugh: it was "totally unreasonable for the bank insurance fund to lead us to believe it is closing anywhere near the insolvent banks in 1990 it should."[24] Several weeks later, he received more ink: "The people are basically in the dark of what I consider to be the 100% probability that taxpayer dollars are going to be needed for the closure of commercial banks."[25]

Suddenly, the healths of the banking industry and the FDIC fund were the focus of widespread concern, reaching in official Washington that apex of attention, the Sunday morning political talk shows. For the nation as a whole, the importance accorded the subjects was evidenced by their consideration on Ted Koppel's *Nightline*. Moderated by Mr. Koppel, Messrs. Seidman and Brumbaugh debated.[26]

Mr. Brumbaugh: "I believe the following banks are very close to true insolvency: Chase, Chemical, Manufacturers Hanover, Bankers Trust, and even Citibank and Bank of America."

. . . . .

Mr. Seidman: "That's irresponsible. It's shouting fire in a crowded theater."

Others were soon contributing their analysis and rhetoric. In August, Salomon Brothers Inc. foresaw a 19 percent drop in the core profits of banks.[27] In September, the General Accounting Office (GAO) pronounced that 35 large banks with aggregate assets of $45.1 billion were "in such severe financial condition" at the end of 1989 as to require recapitalization to prevent failure or forestall federal assistance.[28] Just a day after the GAO pronouncement, the Congressional Budget Office (CBO) projected 631 bank failures costing the FDIC a total of $20.8 billion for 1990 through 1993.[29] Two weeks later, the CBO questioned whether the FDIC could raise premiums enough to rebuild the BIF to 1.25 percent of insured deposits by 1995.[30] In FIRREA, Congress had implicitly suggested 1995 as the date by which the BIF should be at the explicit goal of 1.25 percent of insured deposits.

In early 1991, the Office of Management and Budget was credited with several pessimistic predictions for the BIF: one was a deficit of $22.5 billion by 1995; another was a deficit of $2.2 billion at year-end 1992.[31] The latter prediction was close to a CBO forecast of late January: a $2.8 billion deficit at year-end 1992.[32] The CBO, however, did foresee a return to a positive balance by 1994. In April, the GAO raised the hysteria level by predicting a fund deficit for the current year, 1991, of up to $5 billion.[33] A respected private sector consulting firm, Veribanc, chimed in with the opinion that the BIF was currently insolvent by anywhere from $3.6 billion to $7.6 billion.[34] Ex-Federal Reserve Board Chairman Paul Volcker predicted a taxpayer rescue of the BIF.[35]

The GAO forecast was more than the prattling of an officious bystander. The GAO was the government's auditor. Without a GAO stamp of approval, the FDIC's financial statements would not receive much respect. And as recounted by Mr. Seidman, the GAO was in the process of taking a significantly tougher look at how the FDIC determined the balance in the Bank Insurance Fund.[36] Prior to 1990, the FDIC, in calculating the fund balance, had not attempted to account for potential losses concerning banks that had not yet failed. For the FDIC's 1990 financial statements, however, the GAO was insisting that losses from future failures be taken into consideration. Moreover, in the opinion of Mr. Seidman and the FDIC, the GAO was taking an extremely pessimistic view of how many banks were likely to fail and of what the losses from the failures might ultimately be.

Mr. Seidman and the FDIC battled the GAO throughout the spring and into the summer of 1991. At one point, Mr. Seidman even proposed having GAO personnel accompany FDIC examiners on bank examinations, believing that the experience would reduce the government auditor's level of pessimism. Being an accountant himself, however, Mr. Seidman probably had few illusions about the prospects for successfully arguing with the federal government's number one accountant. In May, the FDIC, partially succumbing to the trend of negative forecasts, foresaw a possible fund balance for year-end 1992 of a minus $4.6 billion.[37] In testimony in June before the House Budget Committee, Mr. Seidman increased the figure to a minus $11 billion, drawing a complaint from Chairman Leon Panetta about the steadily worsening predictions.[38] And in August, the deposit insurer capitulated. It agreed to restate the 1990 fund balance from $8.4 billion to $4.0 billion, thus accepting the GAO's position.[39] Acceptance also carried with it the implication that the fund balance for 1991 would be negative.

The escalating forecasts of a shrinking BIF and the requirement in FIRREA to rebuild the BIF to a reserves-to-insured deposit ratio of 1.25 percent caused the FDIC to consider increases in deposit insurance premiums. FIRREA had mandated a rise in BIF premiums from 8.3 cents per $100 of domestic deposits to 12 cents for 1990 and to 15 cents beginning in 1991. Subject to certain limits, the FDIC could impose higher premiums if the reserve ratio had not reached the 1.25 percent target and was not increasing. In August 1990, the FDIC proposed such a higher premium beginning January 1, 1991: 19.5 cents, or 4.5 cents above the 15 cents that was scheduled to go into effect. The proposed premium was adopted a month later, but it sufficed for only six months. The following April, the FDIC approved a premium of 23 cents, effective July 1.

Even higher rates were suggested. Just before the FDIC's approval of the 23 cents premium in April 1991, the GAO called for a tripling of deposit insurance fees for a year. On top of the 19.5 cents per $100 of domestic deposits, the GAO would have banks pay, for a year, 40 cents per $100 of total *assets*, both domestic and foreign.[40] In May, the CBO ventured that a premium of $1 might be feasible.[41] Mr. Seidman's six–year tenure as chairman of the FDIC came to an end in October. His replacement was William Taylor, who had been staff director of the Federal Reserve Board's Division of Banking Supervision and Regulation. The *American Banker* greeted Mr. Taylor's arrival with the headline, "Boost in FDIC's Premium Rate Moves to Top of Taylor Agenda."[42]

In December 1991, Congress passed and the president signed FDICIA, the Federal Deposit Insurance Corporation Improvement Act. One of the issues during FDICIA's gestation was how to rebuild the BIF. A number of the rebuilding proposals were premised on the belief that raising premiums would not be enough to accomplish the task, at least any time soon. In the end, although the FDIC's borrowing authority from the Treasury was substantially expanded, Congress opted to leave the rebuilding of the deposit insurance funds to premiums, albeit pursuant to a new risk-based premium system. That system and its implementation are described in the next chapter.

THE FAILURES

Underlying the credit crunch debate, the escalating forecasts of the BIF's deterioration, and the increases and suggested increases in deposit insurance premiums was the continuation of the steady stream of bank failures that had been underway for most of the 1980s. For the years 1989 through 1991, the numbers of bank failures were: 1989, 207; 1990, 169; and 1991, 127. The decline in numbers was misleading. The assets of the banks that failed or received assistance from the FDIC totaled $29.2 billion for 1989, $15.7 billion for 1990, and $63.2 billion for 1991. Indeed, in terms of the aggregate assets of banks that failed or received FDIC assistance, 1991 was the all-time high.

Although 1990 was a year of almost consistently bad news about banks, in terms of actual failures it was a bit of a lull. One hundred sixty-nine banks failed, but despite the ruminations of such doomsayers as Mr. Brumbaugh who had contended on *Nightline* that even Citibank and Bank of America were close to insolvency, none of the really big boys went down. The two most notable failures of the year constituted a contrast that, in throwing a bright light on the different possible treatments of floundering institutions, caused defenders of the status quo, including the FDIC, some unease. In August, the National Bank of Washington, with assets of $1.6 billion, was closed. Its assets were purchased and deposits assumed by another Washington, D.C., institution, Riggs National Bank. The deposits included

approximately $33 million at a branch in the Bahamas. The FDIC's staff had rec-
ommended that these deposits, which were uninsured, not be part of the transaction. Chairman Seidman and the FDIC's board, however, overrode the staff.

The contrasting failure was of the Freedom National Bank, New York, in November. With assets of $100 million, this institution was one of the largest African-
American-owned banks in the nation. No purchaser stepped forward as its troubles
reached the critical point, so Freedom was closed and its deposits paid off, which
resulted in losses to uninsured depositors. The explanations of the FDIC and the
other banking regulators about why uninsured depositors who were U.S. citizens
and members of a minority group had to suffer losses but, in the National Bank of
Washington case, uninsured foreign depositors were entitled to full protection were
not particularly persuasive. Many saw the discrepancy in treatment as another example of the unfairness of the alleged too big to fail policy. Congress later provided
compensation to some of the uninsured nonprofit depositors of Freedom.

In early January 1991, the relative lull in bank failures ended with the long-ex-
pected demise of the Bank of New England Corporation. The institution had assets
of $21.7 billion and three principal subsidiaries: Bank of New England, N.A.; Con-
necticut Bank & Trust Company, N.A.; and Maine National Bank. Over a year earlier, in December 1989, the *American Banker*, citing bankers and other analysts,
attributed the Bank of New England's (BNE's) blossoming problems to "a management infatuated with growth and lacking the controls that could have provided
early warnings of potential losses."[43] The article was in response to BNE's
announcement that it was adding over $800 million to its loan loss reserves. The
addition followed a review of the books by bank examiners and was due in large
measure to the institution's heavy exposure to New England's deteriorating real
estate market. Between 1984 and 1989, BNE's real estate loans as a percentage of
all loans had increased from 12 percent to over 30 percent. Before the $800 mil-
lion addition, BNE's reserves amounted to only 39 percent of nonperforming
loans, "the lowest ratio among big commercial banks."[44]

The loan loss addition in December 1989 and the consequent publicity triggered
what amounted to a year-long death watch for BNE. As the time for the
announcement of each quarter's financial results approached, speculation mounted
about how bad the news from BNE would be. Rarely were the pessimists
surprised. Finally in January 1991, the Comptroller of the Currency, as the lead
regulator of BNE's three main subsidiaries, pulled the plug. The FDIC was
appointed receiver and established three bridge banks to which all of the deposits
and most of the assets of the closed institutions were transferred. In July, after a
spirited period of negotiations and bidding, the FDIC awarded the bridge banks to
Fleet/Norstar Financial Group, Providence, Rhode Island. The transaction granted
Fleet/Norstar the right for a limited period to return bad assets to the FDIC.
Moreover, under a service agreement, Fleet/Norstar would manage and liquidate
these returned assets for the deposit insurer. The FDIC estimated that the
transaction would cost it over $1 billion.

Other large institutions followed BNE into the hands of the regulators. In
February, Maine Savings Bank with $1.2 billion in assets was closed. In March, in

acknowledgment of the growth business that closing and disposing of troubled banks had become, the FDIC created a new division, the Division of Resolutions, to centralize responsibilities for bank failures. In May, Goldome, a Buffalo, New York, savings bank with assets of $9.2 billion, was seized. The FDIC estimated it would incur a loss of over $1 billion with respect to Goldome. In August, two Bridgeport, Connecticut, institutions—Citytrust and Mechanics and Farmers Savings Bank (FSB)—were closed. Together, the two institutions had assets of $2.9 billion, and the FDIC estimated the cost of the transaction at $736 million.

In September, another drawn-out high-profile death watch came to its expected conclusion when Southeast Bank, N.A., Miami, Florida, was closed, along with a smaller affiliate.[45] The two institutions had combined assets of $10.8 billion. Southeast had lost nearly $500 million over the previous seven quarters—almost two years—mostly due to real estate lending. The FDIC had been peddling the organization for months. Finally, persuaded by the FDIC's willingness to enter into an innovative loss-sharing arrangement, First Union Corporation of Charlotte, North Carolina, agreed to assume the deposits and acquire most of the assets of the failed institutions. Under the loss-sharing provisions, the FDIC would reimburse First Union for 85 percent of the net charge-offs from the failed banks' portfolios over a five–year period. Another innovative aspect of the transaction was that the FDIC acted before Southeast was technically insolvent. For some time, a number of critics had been urging the regulators to respond more aggressively and at an earlier stage to deteriorating banks, and in FDICIA, Congress was to enact this viewpoint into law.[46]

Savings banks were an important component of the banking industry's troubles in New England, and in part for a surprising reason: too much capital.[47] Many savings banks had recently converted from the mutual to the stock form, a process that usually resulted in more capital as managements sought through stock flotations to satisfy the requirements and concerns of regulators. To fulfill the expectations of the new shareholders, managements had to put the capital to work. The throbbing real estate markets of the late 1980s were where much of the capital went, and where much of it disappeared when the markets crashed. The carnage was especially devastating in New Hampshire. With a lax attitude toward building restrictions, the state had offered relatively few obstacles to starry-eyed developers and their money men. In October 1991, seven New Hampshire banks—three commercial banks and four savings bank—with aggregate assets of $4.4 billion were closed. The FDIC grouped the remnants into two franchises and enticed buyers with, among other attractions, loss-sharing agreements.

The last sizeable failure of 1991 also involved a savings bank. In November, the Connecticut Savings Bank, New Haven, with assets of $1.1 billion, was closed. Its acquirer, Centerbank of Waterbury, received the benefit of the by now standard loss-sharing arrangement.

Commercial banks, savings banks, and savings associations were not the only holders of the public's savings that had difficulties in 1991. Rhode Island had a private deposit insurance program for state-chartered credit unions. Like many state-run or state-authorized deposit insurance programs in the nation's history, the

Rhode Island program proved inadequate when times turned bad. Rhode Island had no legal commitment to back the program, whose solvency consequently depended solely on the resources of the insurance fund and its members. In late 1990, widespread troubles among the members surfaced, and the inadequacy of the fund became apparent. Over 25 percent of Rhode Island's citizens held deposits in the affected credit unions, and these worthy individuals were not particularly persuaded by the absence of a legal commitment on the part of the state.[48] They conveyed their unhappiness to their political representatives. Rhode Island's two senators, Democrat Claiborne Pell and Republican John Chafee, commenced an effort that resulted in a provision in FDICIA authorizing a federal guarantee for state borrowings to reimburse credit union depositors. Thus, depositors in privately insured credit unions in Rhode Island were ultimately bailed out by the taxpayers, but only after the difficulties contributed to the spreading impression of a general collapse among the nation's depository institutions.

The years 1990 and 1991 were a period of much travail for U.S. banks and their regulators. Real estate woes, an alleged credit crunch, a disappearing bank insurance fund, and seemingly endless failures persuaded Congress that the federal banking regulators had lost control of the situation. Congress responded with perhaps the foremost attempt in the nation's history to micromanage bank regulation. That effort, the Federal Deposit Insurance Corporation Improvement Act of 1991, and its aftermath are the subjects of the next chapter.

NOTES

1.   Federal Deposit Insurance Corporation, *Annual Report, 1995*, pp. 32–33; John E. Ryan, Deputy and Acting Chief Executive Officer of the RTC, *Testimony before the Subcommittee on General Oversight and Investigation of the Committee on Banking and Financial Services, House of Representatives*, May 16, 1995, p. 15.

2.   If it indeed occurred, the temporary loss of the FDIC's best and brightest might nevertheless have been immaterial. The thesis of this work is that given the excess capacity in the depository institution's industry, an unpleasant shakeout was inevitable. A marginally higher level of energy and competence in the bank regulatory agencies at the peak of the shakeout most likely would have made little difference.

3.   "FDIC Warns of Higher Losses from Real Estate in 4th Quarter," *American Banker*, December 7, 1989, p. 1.

4.   "Banks Binging Despite Realty Hangover," *American Banker*, March 8, 1990, p. 1.

5.   "Behind the Scenes of a Meeting between Business and Regulators," *American Banker*, April 13, 1990, p. 1.

6.   "Northeast Officials Set to Monitor Regulators," *American Banker*, April 20, 1990, p. 1; see Chapter Five, note 55 and accompanying text.

7.   "Comptroller Takes Heat for Economy in Northeast," *American Banker*, April 27, 1990, p. 1.

8.   June 22, 1990, p. 1.

9.   "Fed Survey Confirms Banks Have Tightened Loan Terms," *American Banker*, August 28, 1990, p. 1; "Fed Finds Credit Squeeze Is Continuing to Worsen," *American Banker*, November 20, 1990, p. 1.

10.   "Bush Asks Regulators to Explain Tight Credit," *American Banker*, November 15, 1990, p. 1.

11. "Regulators to Unveil Plan for Easing Credit Crunch," *American Banker*, February 15, 1991, p. 1; "Loan Evaluation Guidelines Issued," *American Banker*, March 4, 1991, p. 1; "Examiners Briefed on New Guidelines," *American Banker*, March 6, 1991, p. 1.

12. *American Banker*, September 30, 1991, p. 1. See also "Credit Crunch Appears Likely to Linger on for Years, Some Say," *The Wall Street Journal*, September 30, 1991, p. A1.

13. "Treasury Unveils Steps to Stimulate Lending," *American Banker*, October 9, 1991, p. 1; "Bush Moves to Relieve 'Credit Crunch,' " *The Wall Street Journal*, October 9, 1991, p. A2.

14. *American Banker*, December 17, 1991, p. 1.

15. *The Wall Street Journal*, April 27, 1993, p. A1.

16. Richard Cantor and John Wenninger, "Perspective on the Credit Slowdown," pp. 3–36, and Ben S. Bernanke, "Credit in the Macroeconomy," *Federal Reserve Bank of New York Quarterly Review* (Spring 1993) pp. 50–70; M. A. Akhtar, "Causes and Consequences of the 1989–92 Credit Slowdown: Overview and Perspective," *Federal Reserve Bank of New York Quarterly Review* (Winter 1993-94), pp. 1–23; Federal Reserve Bank of New York, *Studies on Causes and Consequences of the 1989-92 Credit Slowdown* (1993).

17. Akhtar, p. 5.

18. Ibid., p. 8.

19. David S. Bizer, "Examiners Crunch Credit," *The Wall Street Journal*, March 1, 1993, p. A14. See also by the same author, "Regulatory Discretion and the Credit Crunch," Unpublished paper, April 6, 1993.

20. "Greenspan: Regulators Overreacted," *American Banker*, February 21, 1991, p. 1; "Fed Chairman, Bankers Clash over Crunch," *American Banker*, April 22, 1991, p. 1.

21. "Consultant Sees Peril to 20% of U.S. Banks," *American Banker*, May 23, 1990, p. 1.

22. " '89 Losses Sink FDIC to Low Point," *American Banker*, May 23, 1990, p. 1.

23. "Seidman Sees $2 Billion Loss at FDIC," *American Banker*, August 1, 1990, p. 1; "Bank Fund Loss Put at $3 Billion," *American Banker*, September 28, 1990, p. 1; "FDIC Hikes Loss Forecast to $4 Billion for this Year," *American Banker*, December 12, 1990, p. 1.

24. July 5, 1990, p. 1.

25. "Health of FDIC Being Exposed to the Spotlight," *American Banker*, July 25, 1990, p. 1.

26. Transcript printed in "A Debate on the Solvency of U.S. Banks," *American Banker*, August 6, 1990, p. 5.

27. "Report Sees 19% Drop in Core Profits," *American Banker*, August 21, 1990, p. 1.

28. "GAO Sees FDIC Unprepared for Probable Slew of Failures," *American Banker*, September 12, 1990, p. 1.

29. "Lawmakers Scramble to Boost FDIC Rates," *American Banker*, September 13, 1990, p. 1.

30. "Study Raises Doubts Fees Can Revive FDIC," *American Banker*, September 26, 1990, p. 1.

31. "FDIC Is Said to Forecast $4 Billion Deficit by 1997," *American Banker*, January 25, 1991, p. 1; "Bush Administration Projects Near-Zero Liquidity for FDIC," *American Banker*, February 5, 1991, p. 2.

32. "FDIC Deficit Will Be Manageable, Congressional Budget Office Says," *American Banker*, January 30, 1991, p. 1.

33. "GAO Urges Tripling FDIC Fees for a Year," *American Banker*, April 29, 1991, p.1.

34. "Veribanc Agrees: Bank Fund Broke," *American Banker*, May 7, 1991, p. 2.

35. "Volcker Foresees Taxpayer Rescue of FDIC Fund," *American Banker*, May 9, 1991, p. 1.

36. L. William Seidman, *Full Faith and Credit* (New York: Times Books, 1993), pp. 169–174.

37. "FDIC Outlook on Bank Fund Turns Bearish," *American Banker*, May 30, 1990, p. 1.

38. "Seidman's Views on Fund: Pessimistic or Even Worse," *American Banker*, June 29, 1991, p. 1.

39. "FDIC Bows to GAO on Fund's Audit," *American Banker*, August 26, 1991, p. 1.

40. "GAO Urges Tripling FDIC Fees for a Year," *American Banker*, April 29, 1991, p. 1.

41. "Congress' Budget Unit Says $1 Premium May Be Feasible," *American Banker*, May 7, 1991, p. 1.

42. October 18, 1991, p. 1.

43. "Real Estate Strategy Turned Sour," *American Banker*, December 21, 1989, p. 1.

44. Ibid., p. 23.

45. Southeast Bank of West Florida, Pensacola; for descriptions of the Southeast closure and the acquisition by First Union Corporation, see *American Banker* articles of September 19, 20, and 23, 1991: "First Union Is Apparent Winner of Miami Bank," p. 1; "First Union Bid Wins Ailing Bank in Miami," p. 1; and "First Union Deal Breaks New Ground," p. 1.

46. Moving to resolve banks before they are insolvent is not without its risks. Although the FDIC initially predicted that the Southeast case would cost it $350 million, this turned out not to be the case. As of early 1998, it appeared that Southeast's creditors, although not its stockholders, would be fully reimbursed for their losses.

47. Seidman, p. 161.

48. Ibid., p. 166.

8

FDICIA and Its Aftermath

In February 1991, Secretary of the Treasury Nicholas F. Brady sent Congress a study entitled *Modernizing the Financial System; Recommendations for Safer, More Competitive Banks.* The study was in fulfillment of a requirement in FIRREA, enacted 18 months earlier, that the Treasury Department examine the federal deposit insurance system. Treasury was to do so in consultation with the OCC, the Federal Reserve, the FDIC, the OTS, the National Credit Union Administration, the Office of Management and Budget, and representatives from the private sector.

The study went well beyond the details of the deposit insurance system to consider the health of the depository institutions industry in general. The recommendations fell into four categories. First, nationwide banking, new financial activities, and commercial ownership of banking organizations should be authorized. These measures would increase bank competitiveness. Second, the scope of deposit insurance should be reined in, supervision should be improved by strengthening the role of capital, and a risk-based deposit insurance premium system should be instituted. These steps would reduce taxpayer exposure and address the loss of market discipline. Third, the fragmented regulatory structure system should be streamlined. Fourth, the Bank Insurance Fund had to be recapitalized.

Treasury's reasoning for taking the study beyond the immediate parameters of deposit insurance was evident in the concluding paragraph of the Executive Summary:

All four components of reform are needed to revitalize the nation's banking system. Reining in the overextended scope of deposit insurance, improving regulation, and recapitalizing BIF are insufficient. In the long run, the competitiveness of banking and financial organizations both at home and abroad depends on allowing them to compete efficiently nationwide and in related financial activities. A banking system that is both sound and competitive is crucial to the health of this nation's economy.

In the months that followed, a central focus of the debates in Congress, in the regulatory community, and in the industry was whether indeed reform needed to include a liberalization of the restrictions on the activities of banking organizations.

FDICIA—ISSUES AND DEVELOPMENT

As the 102nd Congress descended on Washington in early 1991, expectations for a major bank reform bill were high. The Treasury study was due in February. The problems of the banking industry and the deterioration of the Bank Insurance Fund were pleading for attention. Proposals for recapitalizing the fund, for reforming the deposit insurance system, and for expanding, or curbing, the powers of banking organizations were emanating from every nook and cranny. The *American Banker* could have saved everyone much effort, however. In a prescient article in December 1990, it gave the odds for various reform proposals: FDIC recapitalization, sure thing; deposit insurance reform, even; services for the poor, even; reform of the regulatory agencies, 3 to 1; and comprehensive activities reform, 10 to 1.[1] The legislation that emerged from Congress almost a year later provided for FDIC recapitalization, deposit insurance reform, and a few provisions that might be classified as services for the poor but no regulatory agency or comprehensive activities reform. The newspaper could legitimately claim a remarkable degree of foresight.

Probably three factors account for the failure of broad banking reform: the perennial inability of the various elements of the banking and financial industries to agree on changes in bank powers; reflection in Congress of the lack of agreement in the industries; and the unceasing flow throughout 1991 of bad news, which served to highlight the need for immediate remedies at the expense of changes with long term, uncertain payoffs.

Deep-seated disagreements in the banking and financial industries had long stymied efforts to relax restrictions on activities, particularly the activities of banking organizations. The insurance industry did not want banks selling or underwriting insurance and over the years was largely successful in keeping them at bay. Less successfully, the securities industry sought to forestall competition from banks in the selling, distributing, and underwriting of securities. Smaller banks opposed larger banks on several important issues. For example, larger banks generally had less restrictive views on interstate banking and affiliations between banks and commercial businesses. These hostilities among various segments of the banking and financial industries were not to be put aside just because a large-scale collapse appeared imminent.

In March 1991 in an article on the impact rifts among trade groups were having on the bank bill, the *American Banker* published a table (Table 8.1) that highlighted the number and variety of viewpoints involved.[2]

The difficulty of reaching a consensus in the face of such a divergence of opinion is understandable. But, an observer might ask, is that not Congress's job, to produce needed legislation even when those affected cannot agree on what the legislation should contain? Perhaps, but Congress's task is easier if it also answers to a constituency beyond those immediately and directly affected. Banking and finance share with certain other fields the attribute that relatively few outside the industry care. Indeed, relatively few have much understanding of who the players in the nation's banking and financial arenas are, what they do, and how they interact. Thus the players themselves—the members of the industries—are the principal voices that Congress hears, and when the players are divided, Congress hears a cacophony. Moreover, for one reason or another—campaign contributions, former profession, location of a major bank or other financial institution within a congressional district—a member of Congress may have a bias in favor of or against a particular type of player in the banking and financial arenas.

Table 8.1
Trade Group Scorecard: Positions on Bank Reform Plan—How Eleven Trade Groups Stand on Treasury Department Proposals

Treasury Department Proposal	Support	Oppose	No position yet or neutral
Too big to fail	1	8	2
New underwriting powers	6	2	3
New consumer powers	6	1	4
Ownership of banks	3	3	5
Regulatory structure	4	2	5
Brokered deposits	5	1	5
Interstate banking	4	2	5
Capital test	9	0	2
Deposit insurance curbs	1	4	6

In the House of Representatives, FDICIA's development fell under the sway of two such less-than-evenhanded, and exceedingly curmudgeonly, individuals. Initially, House Banking Committee Chairman Henry Gonzalez was in charge. He was an irascible opponent of big banks and the Federal Reserve. From February through June 1991, banking reform wended its way through his committee. The process was not smooth. As the influence of various special interests and trade groups rose and fell, measures were adopted, rejected, and adopted again. Finally, and somewhat surprisingly, a relatively broad bill emerged at the end of June. The bill would permit affiliations not only between banking and securities firms but also between banking and commercial businesses. The bill's margin of victory, however, was narrow: 31 to 20.

Now the second congressman with a pronounced bias entered the picture. The bill was to be reviewed by four other House committees, one of them being Energy and Commerce. Usually some limitations were put on the scope of such secondary reviews. In this case, however, the House leadership gave the secondary reviews virtually free rein.[3] The committees were to decide for themselves what aspects of the bill they wanted to examine. The chairman of the Energy and Commerce

Committee was John Dingell of Michigan. He was just as irascible as Mr. Gonzalez, and Energy and Commerce had jurisdiction over, and consequently a protective attitude toward the securities and insurance fields. He had already attacked the Banking Committee's broad bill,[4] and now he had a mandate to do something about it.

Meanwhile, the Senate was about to take up banking reform in earnest. The chairman of the Senate Banking Committee was Donald Riegle of Michigan. He was not enamored of the idea of mixing banking and commerce, but he did favor a greater degree of interstate banking and a liberalization of the Glass-Steagall restrictions on the separation of commercial and investment banking. As a whole, his committee was probably more attuned to comprehensive reform than he was.

Mr. Dingell showed just how outspoken and contentious he could be when, at a committee session in late July 1991, he charged that Citicorp, the nation's largest banking organization, was insolvent.[5] A Citicorp spokesman responded that the charge was "irresponsible and untrue," and FDIC Chairman Seidman agreed. Mr. Dingell and Mr. Gonzalez commenced what was to be a three month effort to find common ground. They found it, largely where Mr. Dingell stood, although Mr. Gonzalez had never been a great fan of expanding banks' powers and consequently might not have been the most ardent defender of the Banking Committee's position. An *American Banker* headline in mid-September told the tale: "It's the Dingell Bill Now, and Bankers Hate It."[6] Indeed, not only were the provisions expanding the powers of banks being stripped, insurance industry lobbyists were having some success in seeking the curtailment of banks' existing insurance powers, and stronger barriers between banks and securities affiliates were being pressed. Supporters of comprehensive reform, including the Bush administration, had to shift from an offensive strategy aimed at gaining new powers for banks to a defensive one designed to protect existing powers. The Dingell-Gonzalez compromise went before the full House at the end of October and reflected the efforts of advocates of new restrictions on banks. Opponents were able eventually to salvage the status quo: the bill that went to the House-Senate conference committee on November 25, 1991, was mostly devoid of provisions on bank powers.

In the Senate, comprehensive reform had a similar fate. Initially, proponents of a broad bill had some success in moving Senator Riegle toward their position. By early August, however, the American Bankers Association was threatening to withdraw its support for the Senate bill because of possible restrictions on insurance activities and requirements for new services to the poor.[7] The Senate spent most of the fall watching the exuberance with which the House tried not only to scale back comprehensive reform but to add new restrictions on banks. The Senate bill that finally went to the conference committee on November 25 was a bit broader than the House bill—primarily because of an interstate banking measure—but a far cry from what the Bush administration had proposed in February 1991.

So if comprehensive reform had been jettisoned, what actually went to the conference committee? Principally BIF recapitalization and deposit insurance reform measures. For the most part, these topics had not been the subjects of ideological bloodletting—quibbling yes, bloodletting no. Recapitalization was generally considered to be imperative, and only a few contested the notion that the apparently escalating troubles required a significant tightening of the bank supervision and deposit insurance systems.

Recapitalization involved questions of who and how. Some argued that the condition of the BIF was so poor and the ability of banks to rebuild the fund so uncertain that a direct infusion from the taxpayers was necessary. The banking industry resisted this approach, however. The industry prided itself on its alleged independence from the government, conveniently ignoring that without the government's implicit, and for some purposes explicit, backing, banks would likely be in far direr straights than they were. In the opinion of many bankers, an infusion of government money would forever taint the industry, preventing it from saying, "we pay our own way; we protect ourselves; we're not a burden on the taxpayer." In addition, in spite of the industry's seemingly precarious position, not everyone agreed that an immediate infusion of funds was necessary.

The recapitalization options that received the most consideration involved increases and expansions in the FDIC's borrowing authority, which was $5 billion from the Treasury. The industry was even willing to participate. In February 1991, a group of trade associations proposed a plan for the BIF to borrow up to $10 billion as needed by issuing bonds. Through assessments, banks would provide funds to repay the principal and interest on the bonds. In return, banks wanted a cap of 19.5 cents on regular assessment premiums. The plan also called for $2 billion in bank reserves held by the Federal Reserve to be earmarked for an early intervention fund.[8] FDIC Chairman Seidman came forth with his own plan in March. It involved immediate borrowing, an increase in the line of credit with the Treasury, authorization to borrow from commercial banks and the Federal Reserve and to issue preferred and possibly other forms of stock, and increases in insurance premiums.[9] Overall, it would allow the FDIC to borrow as much as $30 billion. Other proposals suggested different borrowing sources—for example, the Federal Reserve Banks.[10] Nevertheless, an increase in the borrowing authority from the Treasury was a component of most proposals and was a major element in the recapitalization eventually specified in FDICIA.

Regarding deposit insurance reform, a number of proposals, some of them quite radical, were advanced in the 1989 to 1991 period. The American Bankers Association focused on the "too big to fail" situation. In essence, it wanted to eliminate too big to fail by having in place a system to provide uninsured depositors and other creditors with immediate settlements based on the FDIC's historic loss experience. The increased certainty such a system would foster supposedly would reduce the possibility of stampedes from an institution in difficulty. A target of several proposals was the $100,000 deposit insurance limit. The Minneapolis Federal Reserve Bank wanted to fully insure just the first $10,000 of a deposit. Insurance would cover 90 percent of the remainder. The reduced insurance coverage would allegedly increase market discipline. The Independent Bankers Association of America leaned in the opposite direction. It proposed that all deposits be insured. One rationale was that too big to fail was not likely to be eliminated, so full insurance was the only way to treat large and small banks equitably.[11]

Capital was considered to be the key by many regulators, policy–makers, and members of the industry. Low capital ratios were viewed as both a symptom and a cause of the current banking difficulties. The Conference of State Bank Supervisors, among others, proposed reduced insurance premiums for banks with high capital levels and strong examination ratings.

The more radical deposit insurance reform proposals involved insurance privatization and the concept of narrow banking. Lowell L. Bryan of McKinsey & Company proposed the privatization of the FDIC and argued that banks should be limited to the business of "core banking."[12] Consultant Bert Ely espoused a private sector cross-guarantee concept as a replacement for federal deposit insurance and as a means for privatizing banking regulation. Charles W. Calomiris of Northwestern University recommended the establishment of a deposit insurance system designed around (1) self-regulation by member institutions and (2) coinsurance.[13] Stephen F. LeRoy of University of California and a visiting scholar at the Federal Reserve Bank of San Francisco suggested that a mutual insurance scheme was workable.[14] Robert E. Litan of the Brookings Institutions proposed a narrow banking concept in which the deposit-taking and lending operations of a financial holding company would be separated.[15] James B. Burnham suggested that narrow banks could hold Federal Reserve deposits, deposits of other banks, U.S. government securities, and most government agency securities.[16] James L. Pierce of the University of California at Berkeley argued that separating the functions banks perform would result in a more stable payments system, which would be the province of narrow banks, and in smoother operating credit markets.[17]

Such proposals had been made before and were to be made after the 1989–1991 period, but the proposals made during that time of troubles had a wider and particularly attentive audience. Nevertheless, the uncertainties of insurance privatization and the extensive industry restructuring that would likely result from the adoption of a narrow banking concept appealed mostly to those academics and consultants who were not burdened with the responsibility to make the real world work. The banking industry might not be in the best of shape, but neither Congress nor the administration nor the regulators were ready to throw out the baby with the bathwater. Deposit insurance reform would be significant but would be limited to the more mundane end of the spectrum.

FDICIA—THE LAW

Most of the disagreements on recapitalization and deposit insurance reform issues had been resolved before the House-Senate conference committee commenced work on November 25. The committee came to quick agreement on a bill focused on recapitalization and deposit insurance reform and that contained no expansion of bank powers and even something of a retreat: state-chartered banks generally were barred from exercising powers not available to national banks. This restraint was a victory for the insurance industry as it negated the laws of several states allowing state banks to conduct insurance underwriting activities. The House adopted the measure on the 26th, the Senate on the 27th—the day before Thanksgiving. President Bush, although expressing unhappiness with the result, signed FDICIA into law on December 19, 1991. On recapitalization, FDICIA increased the FDIC's borrowing authority from the Treasury from $5 billion to $30 billion. Treasury borrowings could be used to cover insurance losses. The Omnibus Budget Reconciliation Act of 1990 had permitted the FDIC to borrow from the Federal Financing Bank for working capital purposes. This was estimated to provide a further $40 billion in borrowing authority. The BIF could also borrow from its member banks, but the amount borrowed would be counted against the $30 billion Treasury limit.[18] Other than what might be drawn under the FDIC's increased borrowing authority, FDICIA provided for no immediate injection of capital into the BIF. Borrowings not repaid by proceeds from the sale of assets were expected to be repaid from the insurance premiums assessed on banks. The FDIC was required to establish an assessment schedule sufficient both to repay any borrowings and to rebuild the BIF within 15 years to a level of $1.25 for each $100 of insured deposits.

The deposit insurance reform measures amounted to a significant tightening of bank supervision. The measures increased the role of capital and reduced considerably regulatory discretion. One item not touched was the $100,000 insurance limit. This had apparently become too sacrosanct. The three main elements of the new supervisory system were prompt corrective action, least-cost resolution, and risk-based assessments.

Prompt corrective action established five capital categories for banks and thrifts: well capitalized, adequately capitalized, undercapitalized, significantly undecapitalized, and critically undercapitalized.[19] The agencies were to set the levels for the capital ratios for the five categories, with the exception of a statutorily prescribed minimum level: tangible equity had to be at least 2 percent of total assets. An institution that fell below this minimum was critically undercapitalized. The three undercapitalized categories carried increasing restrictions. For example, institutions in the undercapitalized category were subject to asset growth limitations. A critically undercapitalized institution was to be placed in receivership unless its regulatory agency, with the concurrence of the FDIC, was convinced it could recover. The significance of requiring a receivership for an institution in the critically undercapitalized category was that it still might have net worth. If its capital ratio was below 2 percent but above zero, it was not insolvent in an accounting sense, and insolvency was the normal test for determining whether a business was bankrupt. Congress's desire to have banks closed before they became insolvent was further evidenced by an early resolution provision in which the banking agencies were encouraged to pursue early resolution strategies.[20]

Least-cost resolution, the second main element of the new supervisory system, replaced the cost test as the criterion the FDIC was to apply in determining how to handle a failed or failing institution.[21] Under the cost test, the FDIC had been able to provide merger assistance if the assistance did not exceed what would have been required to liquidate the institution. An "essentiality" exception allowed the FDIC to ignore the cost-of-liquidation limitation in appropriate cases. Under the more restrictive least-cost test, the FDIC would have to choose the least costly method of handling a failed or failing bank. To try to get a grip on the too big to fail problem, Congress established a difficult-to-trigger systemic risk exception. A least-cost resolution can be foregone—and by implication a resolution method selected that results in uninsured depositors and other creditors being protected—only if the Board of Directors of the FDIC, the Board of Governors of the Federal Reserve System, and the secretary of the Treasury, in consultation with the president, determine the least-costly approach "would have serious adverse effects on economic conditions or financial stability." In a resolution under the systemic risk exception, the portion of the cost above the cost of the least-costly resolution method is to be met by a special assessment on the banking industry.

The third main element of the new supervisory system was risk-based assessments. FDICIA mandated risk-based insurance assessments in an effort to push banks away from riskier activities and conduct. The FDIC was required to institute a risk-based system by 1994, two years away. In devising the system, the FDIC was to consider the risks attributable to different categories of assets and liabilities.

FDICIA buttressed prompt corrective action, least-cost resolution, and risk-based assessments with other changes in bank supervision. Annual on-site examinations were mandated for all banks except for well-managed, well-capitalized ones with assets of under $100 million, which were to be examined every 18 months. The banking agencies were to prescribe, for insured institutions and their holding companies, safety and soundness standards relating to internal controls, loan documentation, credit underwriting, interest rate exposure, asset growth, and compensation, fees, and benefits.[22] The agencies were to revise their risk-based capital standards to take adequate account of interest rate risk, credit risk, and the risk of nontraditional activities.[23] Henceforth, only well-capitalized banks could accept brokered deposits.

The totality of the changes, of which the ones mentioned do not constitute a complete list, pushed bank supervision to a new extreme of micromanagement. Believing that inadequate supervision was a cause of the industry's difficulties, Congress set forth in detail how the banking agencies were to do many aspects of their jobs. One of the main tasks of the agencies over the next several years was to grind out regulations implementing Congress's desires and philosophy.

RISK-BASED ASSESSMENTS

Among the major items that the FDIC had to implement were risk-based assessments. The agency also had to ensure that assessments were sufficient to restore the Bank Insurance Fund to a ratio of 1.25 percent of insured deposits within 15 years.

Since July 1991, the assessment rate had been 23 cents per $100 of domestic deposits. As a result of the Omnibus Budget Reconciliation Act of 1990 and FDICIA, the FDIC had virtually unlimited theoretical authority to increase assessment rates to meet the BIF's obligations and to repay any Treasury borrowings. FDICIA required the FDIC to implement a risk-based assessment system by 1994, but the apparently exigent condition of the BIF persuaded many observers that the agency should take earlier action under its broad assessment power. One proponent of earlier action was the FDIC's new chairman, Bill Taylor. Persuaded in part by a jump of 26 percent in the size of the FDIC's problem bank list—not in terms of the number of banks on the list but in terms of the assets of banks on the list—he wanted an increase in premiums as early as mid-1992.[24] A good portion of the banking industry, however, did not see the urgency, or at least viewed the urgency as mitigated by the cost of increased premiums. These opponents mounted a campaign to ward off an increase.[25] The targets were the other four members of the FDIC's Board of Directors.

Two of the board members were within the Treasury Department and consequently were part of the Administration: Director of the Office of Thrift Supervision Timothy Ryan and Acting Comptroller of the Currency Stephen Steinbrink. Absent strongly held views of their own, they could be persuaded to accommodate the administration's wishes, and bankers soon had the administration wishing for, at the very least, no midyear premium increase. The other two directors were C. C. Hope, Jr., and Andrew C. "Skip" Hove, Jr., who was also the FDIC's vice chairman. Both former bankers with strong ties to the industry, they could be counted on to accord industry views careful consideration. But they weren't pushovers.

Maneuvering on the timing and form of an assessment change was heavy in the first months of 1992. Details of a compromise began to surface in April. Chairman Taylor had not been able to secure agreement on a midyear increase, but he did gain the support of Directors Hope and Hove for putting a risk-based system into effect on January 1, 1993, a year earlier than required by FDICIA.[26] By a 3-to-2 vote in May, the FDIC's Board of Directors formally put the proposal for a preliminary system out for a 60–day comment period (see Table 8.2). By constructing a matrix of three supervisory ratings—healthy, supervisory concern, and substantial supervisory concern—and three capital ratings—well capitalized, adequately capitalized, and less than adequately capitalized—the FDIC produced nine assessment, or premium, possibilities. The premiums ranged from 25 cents to

Table 8.2
Risk-based Assessment Schedule (Per $100 of insured deposits)—Proposed May 1992

	Healthy	Supervisory concern	Substantial supervisory concern
Well capitalized	$.25	$.28	$.30
Adequately capitalized	$.28	$.30	$.30
Less than adequately capitalized	$.30	$.30	$.31

31 cents per $100 of insured deposits. The FDIC estimated that the average premium would be 28 cents, which was a 22 percent increase over the existing single premium of 23 cents. A 22 percent increase was how the proposal came to be characterized in the debates of the next few months.

Two factors derailed the adoption of the assessment schedule as proposed. First, as discussed later in this chapter, the banking industry was in the process of putting together the, until then, most profitable year in its history, and the BIF was rapidly erasing its $7 billion deficit of year-end 1991. Not many were noticing the recoveries, but among the few who were paying attention were bankers with sufficient clout to persuade the administration to resist a premium increase even more than it had in the spring.

The second factor was the unexpected death of Bill Taylor. He entered the hospital on August 12 for what was reported as uncomplicated surgery. Following what seemed to be a successful operation, he contracted pneumonia, and died on August 20. He was 53 years old. The *American Banker* wasted little time in draping the tragedy with the typical Washington priorities. Under the headline reporting Chairman Taylor's death was the sub-headline: "Premium Rise Now in Doubt."[27]

Table 8.3
Risk-based Assessment Schedule (Per $100 of insured deposits)—Adopted September 1992

	Healthy	Supervisory concern	Substantial supervisory concern
Well capitalized	$.23	$.26	$.29
Adequately capitalized	$.26	$.29	$.30
Less than adequately capitalized	$.29	$.30	$.31

And indeed it was. As the vice chairman, Skip Hove was now the acting chairman of the FDIC. He had voted in May for the proposed schedule and its increase, but he was not thought to be as emphatic about the matter as Mr. Taylor ad been.[28] Moreover, the FDIC's board no longer had a majority in favor of the increase as proposed in May. With Mr. Taylor gone, the board was split 2–to–2. A vote on the proposal had been scheduled for late August, but at the insistence of the administration's representatives on the Board—Messrs. Ryan and Steinbrink—action was postponed for two weeks. The Administration used the delay to send a message. In its September 3 issue, the *American Banker* had an article headlined, "Bush Weighed Plan to Pack FDIC Board." The article said that the administration had considered several ways of replacing Mr. Hove as acting chairman and thereby creating a 3–to–2 administration majority. Mr. Hove, who had been a naval aviator in his youth, was the quintessential country banker, and appeared to have no ambitions for a brighter niche in Washington's firmament, was not likely intimidated. But he also did not have the votes for a sizeable premium increase even if he were inclined in that direction.

The outcome was that in mid-September a risk-based schedule with a range of 23 cents to 31 cents was adopted (see Table 8.3). Thus the lowest category, in which 75 percent of the nation's banks were located, had no premium change from the existing flat-rate 23 cents. The FDIC estimated that the average premium would rise to 25.4 cents. The smallness of the increase was seen as a victory for the banking industry and, in the typical Washington view of decisions as no more than the keeping of score in a power struggle, as a "capitulation" to the Bush administration.[29] Congressional Democrats were perturbed. The schedule, however, was to prove more than enough to rebuild the BIF, and far ahead of the 15-year timetable specified in FDICIA.

FAILURES

Statistically, 1992 was an impressive year for bank failures. For the eighth consecutive year, more than 100 banks failed or were assisted. The 122 cases were only three less than in 1991. More significantly, the amount of assets in the failed or assisted banks, $44.2 billion, was second only to 1991, the all-time high for bank failures measured in terms of the assets involved. But often situations, events, and happenings are judged relatively rather than absolutely. Expectations at the beginning of 1992 were for the most part extremely pessimistic. As the year went by and fewer banks were closed than expected, complaints were uttered that the FDIC and the other regulators were being too lax. It being an election year, politics were suspected, as chronicled in the next section of this chapter.

January belied the letdown that the year was to become for aficionados of disaster. In that month, the FDIC placed Crossland Savings, FSB, with $8.7 billion in assets, into conservatorship. The agency had been unable to find a buyer for the Brooklyn, New York, institution and decided to attempt the controversial approach of nursing it along until a buyer appeared. Commentators talked of a bank "hospital," some favorably, some unfavorably, and of a new tact in bank resolutions. In truth, Crossland turned out to be a unique, and incidently largely successful, effort. It was sold by the FDIC in 1993 to institutional investors.

Also in January, the FDIC closed Independence Bank of Encino, California, a subsidiary of the notorious Bank of Credit and Commerce International (BCCI), a foreign holding company that regulators abroad and in the United States had closed in 1991. BCCI had pled guilty to illegal ownership of U.S. financial institutions, fraud, racketeering, and money laundering. The payoff of Independence Bank was one of the largest payoffs in the FDIC's history. Unlike in most deposit payoffs, however, all deposits, not just insured deposits, were fully paid off. The reason for the full compensation was that the FDIC expected to be fully reimbursed from a special fund established from BCCI assets.

In February, a small but noteworthy, precedent-setting resolution occurred. Landmark Bank of Fort Worth, Texas, with assets of $82.8 million, was closed. In a purchase and assumption transaction, its insured deposits and a portion of its assets were acquired by Central Bank and Trust Company, Fort Worth. Central did not assume approximately $429,000 in 21 accounts that exceeded the deposit insurance limit of $100,000. This determination not to protect uninsured deposits in a P&A transaction was the first such decision by the FDIC and was prompted by FDICIA's passage two months earlier. Although full implementation of FDICIA's stricter resolution criteria and procedures was not required until January 1, 1995, the FDIC was off to an early start. "P&As-insured deposits only" were to be used for 42 transactions during the year.

In another type of action prompted by FDICIA's underlying philosophy of increased strictness, in October the FDIC arranged for the resolution of two institutions before their book capital had been depleted. The institutions were the Howard Savings Bank, Newark, New Jersey, with assets of $3.6 billion, and First Constitution Bank, New Haven, Connecticut, with assets of $1.6 billion.

Three other large savings banks, in addition to Crossland, Howard, and First Constitution, were the subjects of resolutions during the year: Dollar Dry Dock Bank, White Plains, New York, with assets of $3.8 billion, in February; American Savings Bank, White Plains, New York, with assets of $3.2 billion, in June; and Meritor Savings Bank, Philadelphia, Pennsylvania, with assets of $3.6 billion, in December. In each instance, the bank was closed and the deposits assumed and certain of the assets acquired by another institution. All the deposits of Dollar and Meritor were assumed, but the American transaction was a P&A-insured deposits only: the uninsured deposits of American were not transferred to the acquiring institution.

Finally, in October 1992, First City Bancorporation of Texas was resolved for the second time, the first having occurred in 1988 when the FDIC provided a $970 million assistance package to new owners. In 1992 the FDIC closed 20 First City banking subsidiaries, with $8.8 billion in assets, and established 20 full-service bridge banks. Sixteen of the bridge banks assumed all the deposits in the 16 better-capitalized closed subsidiaries. For the four largest subsidiaries, only insured deposits were transferred. Customers with deposits in excess of the insurance limit at those four subsidiaries received an advance dividend equal to 80 percent, shortly increased to 90 percent, of their uninsured claims. In January 1993, the FDIC announced the sale of the 20 bridge banks to various acquirers.

FORECASTS AND POLITICS

The enactment of FDICIA did not halt the dire forecasts that had dominated 1990 and 1991. In late December 1991, consultant Karen Shaw was quoted as opining that a premium of 35 to 40 cents per $100 of insured deposits would be necessary to cover losses from failed banks and to rebuild the BIF to the target ratio of 1.25 percent of insured deposits. In the same article, an unnamed Citicorp analyst said premiums would have to range between 28 to 40 cents for fifteen years.[30]

In March 1992, the Office of Management and Budget, influenced by a jump in the assets of banks on the FDIC's problem bank list from $487 billion in September 1991 to $613 billion in January 1992, foresaw "giant" bank failures.[31] Not to be outdone, in April the Congressional Budget Office raised by $13 billion the losses it had projected the previous August for the 1992–95 time period. The new projection was $40 billion, and the number of failed banks for the four years was forecast as 719.[32] If the insurance assessment were raised to 27 cents, the CBO's analysis showed that the BIF would still be $12 billion in the red in 1997.

Also in April, election year politics began to intrude on the forecasting business. The *American Banker* noted that the number of bank closings in the year were thus far less than expected.[33] The usual experts were paraded out. Karen Shaw was suspicious: "The numbers suggest something is going on." CBO Director Robert D. Reischauer, in a less-than-evenhanded remark unusual for an occupant of his position, stated that "we may have to call in a rocket scientist to explain" the few resolutions in the election years of 1988 and 1992. Later in the month, the always gloomy Ed Kane expressed his unhappiness with the FDIC's hesitancy in adopting an assessment increase: "The FDIC is about $50 billion under water today."[34]

In June, the FDIC proposed the 15-year BIF recapitalization schedule required by FDICIA. The projection had the BIF in negative numbers through 1999. Banks holding about $506 billion, or 15 percent of the industry's assets, were expected to fail between 1992 and 2006. Although most of the failures were predicted to occur between 1992 and 1995, the FDIC had banks holding between $20 billion and $28 billion going under each year between 1996 and 2006. Another variable influencing the recapitalization was the insurance assessment. The FDIC had the assessment at 28 cents per $100 of deposits through 1997—the projection was made before the FDIC adopted the assessment schedule in September that increased the average assessment to 25.4 cents. In the June projection, the assessment would fall to 26 cents in 1998 and 24 cents in 2001. The *American Banker* noted that Chairman Taylor "was obviously uncomfortable committing the agency to such a long forecast." FDIC research director Roger Watson characterized the effort as "a synthesis of everyone's perceptions" rather than a projection of what was going to happen over the 15 years.[35]

Talk of a "December surprise" began to mount in the summer of 1992 as the banking agencies readied regulations implementing FDICIA's prompt corrective action provisions. Prompt corrective action (PCA) was to go into effect in December and in general would require the closure of critically undercapitalized banks—those with capital-to-assets ratios of under 2 percent. Estimates varied as to how big an immediate impact PCA would have. One set of observers foresaw a considerable impact and moreover contended that the banking regulators and the administration were downplaying—the most vehement used harsher terms such as covering up—the likely consequences; hence the "December surprise."

The pessimistic outcries came to a head shortly before the November election and probably contributed to the general unease that cost George Bush a second term. A recession had stretched from July 1990 to March 1991. It was over long before the election in November 1992, but that fact was apparent only in hindsight. Indeed, the Democrats were successful in convincing a necessary proportion of the electorate that hard times were still at hand. "It's the economy, stupid," was the slogan of the campaign of Arkansas's William Jefferson Clinton, never mind that the economy was actually on the rebound. News about difficulties in the banking industry comported nicely with the notion that the economy, in general, was in trouble.

In mid-October 1992, *The Washington Post* published a book, *Banking on the Brink*, by two relative novices to the field of commentary on banking. The two were Edward W. Hill, a professor at Cleveland State University, and Robert J. Vaughan, a consultant. They presented a range of scenarios for the banking industry, with the most pessimistic scenario entailing over 1,000 bank failures and a cost to the BIF of almost $100 billion. Critics and supporters alike focused on the pessimistic scenario, and the debate raged. In fact, the matter hit the presidential debates. On the evening of October 19, candidates Bush, Clinton, and Ross Perot, gave their views on the apparent troubles in the banking industry. President Bush and Governor Clinton were relatively low-key, acknowledging that some weak banks existed but discounting the possibility of widespread problems. Mr. Perot, however, was not restrained:

Now if you believe *The Washington Post* and you believe this extensive study that's been done—and I'm reading—right after election day this year they're going to hit us with 100 banks—it'll be a $100 billion problem.

Now if that's true, just tell me now. Yeah, I'm grown up, I can deal with it, I'll pay my share. But just tell me now. Don't bury it until after the election twice [apparently referring to 1988]. I say that to both political parties. The people deserve that since we have to pick up the tab. You got the PAC money, we'll pay the tab. Just tell us.[36]

To investigate—maybe for political purposes, maybe out of true concern—the possibility of a "December surprise," the chairman of the Senate Banking Committee, Democrat Donald Riegle, called an election eve hearing. Most private sector witnesses foresaw some degree of taxpayer bailout. Dan Brumbaugh, for example, said: "In my personal opinion, I do believe there is going to be a taxpayer bailout." He did not think, however, that there would be a December surprise.[37] Another chronic naysayer chimed in through a column in the *American Banker*. Martin Mayer also did not expect a December surprise. "It is not impossible, however, that we will begin seeing some surprises as early as January and all but certain that we will have some bad news in late 1993 and 1994, when interest rates turn up again."[38]

Messrs. Brumbaugh's and Mayer's predictions of no December surprise were accurate. Their forecasts of later difficulties were far off the mark, however. Unforeseen by almost everyone who ventured a public opinion, U.S. banks were at the threshold of a period of prosperity unmatched in the modern history of the industry.

RECOVERY

For the banking industry, 1992 was a year that the rhetoric did not match the reality. What with the dire forecasts and the talk of a "December surprise," and against the background of the Democrats' "It's the economy, stupid," the rhetoric was decidedly negative. The reality was that the industry was rather quietly putting together the until then most profitable year in its history, and the FDIC, even under the GAO's very conservative accounting standards, was adding just short of $7 billion to the bank deposit insurance fund, bringing the fund from a minus $7 billion to almost a positive balance.

A major ingredient in the performance of both the banking industry and the economy was the monetary policy moves of the Federal Reserve. In response to the faltering economy, the Fed began easing money market conditions in late 1990 and continued easing through 1991 and 1992. From a peak of 9.85 percent in March 1989, the federal funds rate, a principal monetary policy target, declined to 6.91 percent in January 1991, 4.43 percent in December 1991, and 2.92 percent in December 1992. In a series of steps, the Fed reduced the discount rate, the rate the Federal Reserve banks charge for short term borrowings by member institutions, from 7.0 percent in December 1990 to 3.0 percent in July 1992. For both rates, the levels were the lowest that had been seen since the 1960s.[39] By 1992, the economic recovery from the recession of July 1990–March 1991 was underway, but the fact was not generally appreciated.

Buried in the largely negative commentary about the banking industry in 1992 were tidbits of optimism. In June, the FDIC reported that commercial banks earned a record $7.6 billion in the first quarter. Chairman Taylor was cautious, attributing the performance to low interest rates and one-time gains on the sale of securities.[40] Net income in each of the next two quarters was higher still, and in the third quarter the number of banks on the FDIC's "problem bank" list fell below 1,000 for the first time since 1985. By December, in an article assessing FDICIA one year after its enactment, the *American Banker* was ready to reevaluate the situation: "Were the FDIC's problems exaggerated? Increasingly, it appears that the answer is yes."[41]

In March 1993, the full picture of the industry's year following FDICIA became clear when the FDIC released 1992 performance statistics. Commercial banks had earned a record $32.2 billion. The previous high had been $24.8 billion in 1988. The average return on assets was 0.96 percent, the highest level since the creation of the FDIC. Only two of the 25 largest banks lost money, compared with 7 in 1991.[42] More good news came two months later when the FDIC announced that the BIF had almost eliminated its negative balance of $7 billion. Its year-end 1992 balance was a negative $100.6 million.

The banking industry's performance in 1992 was not an aberration. Indeed, the industry was embarked on a period of prosperity that was still underway in 1998. Profits each year succeeded the previous year's. In 1993, industry return on accounts (ROA) achieved an historic high, 1.20 percent. ROA for the next three years was only marginally lower, 1.15 percent in 1994, 1.17 percent in 1995, and 1.19 percent in 1996. For 1997, ROA set another record, 1.23 percent. Industry annual net income for 1996 exceeded $50 billion for the first time, and for 1997 was $59.2 billion. The FDIC's Bank Insurance Fund went along for the ride. In May 1995, the fund reached the designated target ratio 1.25 percent of insured deposits, 11 years ahead of the 15-year recapitalization period Congress had specified in FDICIA. The FDIC reduced assessments for BIF-insured institutions to an average to 4.4 cents per $100 of insured deposits for the second half of 1995 and to an average of just 0.3 cents beginning in 1996. For the first six-month assessment period in 1996, approximately 93 percent of BIF-insured institutions paid the statutory minimum assessment of $1,000.

And did the General Accounting Office, the Office of Management and Budget, the Congressional Budget Office, and the other predictors of gloom eat public crow?[43] Not to the extent that very many noticed. Reasons can always be found as to why one's forecast does not come to pass. Besides, other things to rail against are forever appearing.

Will the good times continue into the next millennium? That is a topic considered as part of the assessment in the final chapter.

NOTES

1. "Congress to Push Broad Banking Reform," *American Banker*, December 19, 1990, p. 1.

2. "Trade Group Rift May Stall Reform Bill," *American Banker*, March 1, 1991, p. 1.

3. "Rep. Foley Deals Blow to Treasury Reform Bill," *American Banker*, July 24, 1991, p. 1.

4. "Rep. Dingell Attacks Bid to Broaden Bank Powers," *American Banker*, July 11, 1991, p. 1.

5. "Dingell Slams Bank Bill, Calls Citicorp 'Insolvent,' " *American Banker*, August 1, 1991, p. 1.

6. *American Banker*, September 18, 1991, p. 1.

7. "ABA May Pull Support for a Major Overhaul," *American Banker*, August 6, 1991, p. 1.

8. "Industry Plan on Insurance Is Unveiled," *American Banker*, February 13, 1991, p. 2.

9. "FDIC Proposes to Borrow as Much as $30 Billion," *American Banker*, March 1, 1991, p. 1.

10. "Fed Banks Would Refinance FDIC under Bush Bill," *American Banker*, March 19, 1991, p. 1.

11. See "Deposit Insurance Reform Draws a Crowd," *American Banker*, March 6, 1990, p. 1.

12. Lowell L. Bryan, "A Blueprint for Financial Performance," *Harvard Business Review* (May–June, 1991), pp. 73-86; "Core Banking," *McKinsey Quarterly* (1991, No. 1), pp. 61-74; *Bankrupt: Restoring the Health and Profitability of Our Banking System* (New York: Harper Business, 1991).

13. Charles W. Calomiris, "Is Deposit Insurance Necessary? A Historical Perspective," *The Journal of Economic History* (June 1990, Vol. 50, No. 2), pp. 283–295.

14. Stephen R. LeRoy, "Mutual Deposit Insurance?" *FRBSF Weekly Letter*, Federal Reserve Bank of San Francisco (June 8, 1990).

15. Robert E. Litan, *The Revolution in U.S. Finance* (Washington, D.C.: The Brookings Institution, 1991).

16. James B. Burnham, "Deposit Insurance: The Case for the Narrow Bank," *Regulation* (Spring 1991, No. 14), p. 2.

17. James L. Pierce, *The Future of Banking* (New Haven, Conn.: Yale University Press, 1991).

18. Borrowing from BIF members also was restricted by a liability limit: the FDIC's liability for the payment of interest and the repayment of principal was limited to the amount equal to the amount of assessment income received by the BIF from assessments (Pub. L. No. 102–242, section 105).

19. Pub. L. No. 102–242, section 131.

20. Pub. L. No. 102–242, section 143.

21. Pub. L. No. 102–242, section 141; see Chapter 4 for further descriptions of the cost and least-cost tests.

22. Pub. L. No. 102–242, section 132.

23. Pub. L. No. 102–242, section 305.

24 "Sick Banks' Assets Up 26% in Last Four Months," *American Banker,* February 12, 1992, p. 1.

25. See "Big Banks Blame Thrifts for Losses at Bank Fund," *American Banker*, February 19, 1992, p. 2.

26. See the following *American Banker* articles: "Taylor Predicts FDIC Premium Will Rise Soon—'Maybe June,'" December 27, 1991, p. 2; "No Midyear Hike Seen for FDIC Premiums," April 7, 1992, p. 1; "Healthy Banks to Gain Under Premium Plan," April 8, 1992, p. 1; "29–Cent Premium Seen for Half of Banks, S&Ls," April 14, 1992, p. 1; "FDIC Chief Clarifies Plan," April 16, 1992 p. 2; "Trade Groups Lobby to Stop Premium Hike," May 8, 1992, p. 1; "Critics Warn Risk-Based Premiums Would Have Painful Side Effects," May 12, 1992., p. 1.

27. "FDIC Chief Taylor Dead at 53," *American Banker*, August 21, 1991, p. 2.

28. "Interim Chief to Press for Hike in FDIC Fees," *American Banker*, August 27, 1992, p.1.

29 "FDIC Fixes Premium at Average 25.4 Cents," *American Banker*, September 16, 1992, p. 1.

30. "Congress' Rx for Banks: A Fatal Dose?" *American Banker*, December 20, 1991, p. 1.

31. "Budget Office Foresees Giant Bank Failures," *American Banker*, March 9, 1992, p. 1.

32. "CBO Raises Estimate of Losses for FDIC," *American Banker*, April 2, 1992, p. 1.

33. "Administration Denies Delaying Bank Closings," *American Banker*, April 3, 1992, p. 1.

34. "Premium Hike: FDIC 'Wasting Time,'" *American Banker*, April 10, 1992, p. 10.

35. "FDIC Gives Grim Failure Forecast," *American Banker*, June 17, 1992, p. 2.

36 "Text of the Candidates' Give and Take on Banking Issues," *American Banker*, October 21, 1992, p. 10.

37. "FDIC May Not Need Credit Line, Hove Says," *American Banker*, October 27, 1992, p. 1.

38. Martin Mayer, "No 'December Surprise,' but a January Mess," *American Banker*, October 4, 1992, p. 4.

39. Board of Governors of the Federal Reserve System, *Annual Reports.*

40 "Bank Profits Set a Record for Quarter, Rising 36%," *American Banker*, June 11, 1992, p. 1.

41. "As FDIC's Problems Ease, '91 Rescue Second-Guessed," *American Banker*, December 3, 1992, p. 1.

42. Federal Deposit Insurance Corporation, *Quarterly Bank Profile*, 4th Quarter 1992.

43.   The FDIC itself had issued a few predictions of gloom, one of them being the 15-year recapitalization schedule for the BIF required by FDICIA (see text accompanying note 35). The agency, however, had amended the schedule as the remarkable recovery of the banking industry became apparent, although one has trouble finding an explicit, affirmative official admission that the original schedule was just plain wrong.

9

An Assessment

A theme of this work is that the thrift crisis and banking troubles of the 1980s and early 1990s were not primarily due to fraud, deregulation, inadequate supervision, overly exuberant lending, abrupt changes in tax policies, or a host of other short term causes. All of these factors certainly exacerbated, and in some cases triggered, the problems of depository institutions. But the underlying, fundamental reason for the thrift crisis and banking troubles was a form of excess capacity that resulted from many decades of protection from the rigors of competition and the marketplace. The protection was due to geographical and product limitations and a deposit insurance system that became focused on the prevention of failures of individual institutions. By 1980, the depository institutions industry was ripe for a severe culling, a culling that legislators and regulators probably could have done little to avoid, although they might have channeled and controlled it better.

No one individual or group was responsible for the creation of excess capacity over a period of many decades. The industry structure that was poised for a significant restructuring in 1980 was the cumulative result of a thousand decisions, and nondecisions, stretching back to the early days of the nation's existence. The structure reflected the interaction of many diverse attitudes and philosophies. Still, several factors can be singled out as particularly significant in the development of an industry burdened with overcapacity and ready for substantial thinning.

One was the establishment of the federal deposit insurance system. Such a system was not inevitable in 1933. An alternative favored by a number of observers was to allow the banking system to strengthen itself through branching. But branching was opposed by defenders of small community banks, and they carried the day. Thus a government-operated system designed in part to maintain a structurally unconcentrated industry came into being.

A second factor was the degree to which the avoidance of bank failures became a goal of the federal deposit insurance system. Such a goal was a natural outgrowth of a system designed in part to maintain a structurally unconcentrated industry. But a less strenuous defense of the status quo, and a less hostile aversion to bank failures, would seem to have been possible. After all, stripped to its fundamentals deposit insurance was, and is, no more than the government guarantee of the repayment of deposits, up to a certain amount, in a failed bank. Bank failures themselves very shortly became anathemas, however. This together with the hurdles an expansive view of the antitrust laws posed to the combining of neighboring banks rendered structural evolution of the industry extremely difficult.

Finally, some relaxation of product and geographic restrictions occurred in the 1960s and 1970s, but nowhere near enough to prevent the development of too much capacity. Each victory for the supporters of relaxation was hard-fought and time-consuming. The marketplace was moving at a much faster pace. In addition, many proposals never came to fruition or were adopted much too late. For example, the Hunt Commission in 1972 and the FINE study in 1973 recommended that the powers of federal thrifts be expanded.[1] If such deregulation had occurred at the time, the debacle that was triggered when deregulation actually took place under conditions of extreme stress in the early 1980s might have been avoided.

Given that the U.S. depository institutions industry was due for a significant culling by 1980, how well did the industry's regulators respond and how well did the regulatory system measure up? The answers depend on what result is emphasized. On one hand, the nation's banking industry did not collapse. No depositor lost a federally insured deposit, and the losses among uninsured depositors and creditors were relatively light. The nation experienced a recession in 1990–1991. The downturn was far from a depression, however, and could be viewed as a normal blip of the business cycle, or due to the ceaseless restructuring that characterizes a dynamic economy. On the other hand, the costs to the taxpayer to clean up the thrift portion of the depository institutions industry was an estimated $132 billion. Moreover, the ultimate question could always be posed another way: did the banking industry survive because of or in spite of the regulatory system and the actions of the regulators?

The belief here—and it is only a belief, not a matter that can be proved quantitatively—is that the regulatory system was a factor in the survival and reemergence of the banking system, but not at a level where detail is important. The banking industry was not subject to systemic problems, to a public panic and widespread bank runs, because of confidence. The public had confidence that the government was standing behind the banking system. If that confidence had been lacking, can it really be contended that the failures of more than a hundred banks a year for eight years from 1985 through 1992—would have occurred without triggering fears of a general financial collapse? This point seems to have escaped the proponents of several recent proposals that would reduce the government's backing of the banking system.[2] Alterations to improve the regulatory system, including its deposit insurance component, should never be rejected out-of-hand. The degree of the government's direct involvement should be subject to continuous reevaluation. But those who want to reduce the government's ultimate responsibility have an extremely difficult argument to make.

At levels below the macro-performance of the system, levels where details are important, assessing the performance of the regulators regarding the banking difficulties of the 1980s and early 1990s becomes more difficult. The choices made between forbearance—allowing troubled institutions time in which to recover—and strictness, between closing institutions or merging them with healthy ones, between mergers and open bank assistance, are all open to second-guessing. The later arrangements the FDIC made with acquiring institutions concerning who—the FDIC or the acquiring institution—was responsible for bad assets tended to favor the acquiring institutions more than in earlier arrangements. Was this trend in favor of acquiring institutions a necessary or desirable development? Such issues and questions are of interest to those evaluating the actions of the regulators within a given regulatory scheme, and even to an extent to those evaluating the scheme itself. In my view, this level of focus is not particularly relevant to an inquiry into underlying, fundamental causes. The "devil may be in the details," but sometimes to see the overall picture one has to rise above the details. That has been an objective of this work.

Another category of questions that can be posed about the banking troubles ultimately involves the nature of bureaucracies. For 40 years, banking regulators lived a relatively quiet existence. The challenges of crises were few and far between. The status quo was not seriously questioned. As the 1980s dawned, were individuals accustomed to a rather lethargic existence equipped and prepared for the volatility ahead? Perhaps only a social scientist well-versed in the human resources field is capable of venturing authoritative opinions on this subject.

THE FUTURE

What is the future of the banking industry? On the positive side, many of the product and geographic limitations that gave rise to the banking troubles and thrift crisis have been or are being reduced or eliminated. In the 1980s, a number of states allowed out-of-state bank holding companies to acquire in-state banks. And in the Riegle-Neal Interstate Banking and Branching Efficiency Act of 1994, Congress largely removed the remaining barriers to interstate banking operations. The act authorized bank holding companies, beginning September 1995, to acquire banks located in any state. Further, as of June 1, 1997, the act authorized banks to branch across state lines through merger unless a state affirmatively rejected this option prior to that date. Only two states, Montana and Texas, did so, and Texas's rejection expires in 1999. A number of states have gone the minimum federal requirements one better and allowed de novo interstate branching.

Congress has not been as successful in reducing product limitations. The basic federal laws that have contributed to how the various components of the financial industry—banking, securities, and insurance—have evolved remain in place. Efforts to change these laws have been extensive but as of early 1998 not very productive. Nevertheless, as a cumulative result of a number of court decisions and regulatory actions over the years, product limitations are much less pervasive and constraining than they once were. For example, banking organizations can provide securities brokerage services, to a limited extent can underwrite and deal in securities, and can sell some insurance and insurance-type products.

Thus the geographic and product restrictions that gave rise to excess capacity in the banking and financial industries have been substantially reduced. Competition is much freer to perform its beneficial strengthening and culling effects, which should help curtail the development of the speculatory and self-destructive practices that contributed significantly to the problems of the 1980s and early 1990s.

Another positive factor concerning the future of the banking industry is the realization among at least some in the regulatory community that ensuring safety and soundness is a much more complicated business than their predecessors had thought. In 1995, the FDIC established a Division of Insurance (DOI) to identify, analyze, and disseminate information on current and emerging risks to the deposit insurance funds. Among its tasks, DOI is charged with spotting changes in regional economic conditions that might have detrimental impacts on depository institutions. The other bank regulatory agencies have comparable programs underway. With a number of banking organizations, the agencies have also begun taking a broader, more encompassing approach to analyzing the risks faced by individual institutions. Rather than evaluating risks in isolation, banks and the agencies are attempting a portfolio approach in which risks are judged in their totality. These initiatives to better understand and respond to the risks faced by both the industry and individual institutions indicate an inquisitiveness that itself should be a positive factor regarding the future.

On the other hand, the regulatory agencies are probably still too focused on the safety and soundness of individual institutions. The central component of the bank regulatory system is the bank examination. Periodically, a bank is scrutinized in detail by a team of examiners. This on-site examination is in addition to off-site reviews of the financial data that banks must file regularly. The examination system could well foster an overly protective attitude on the part of the regulators toward the regulated. How can examiners not feel a sense of responsibility if an institution they recently examined goes under? Many observers, including more than a few members of Congress, equate a failure of a bank with the failure of bank regulators to do their job. It is pointing out the obvious to say that bank regulators do not like to offend members of Congress.

Thus the bank regulatory system, with the on-site examination as its pillar, arguably creates a bias against the failure of individual institutions. Yet if the thesis of this work is correct, the paucity of the failure of individual institutions contributes to the conditions that eventually threaten the failure of the industry. Ricki Helfer, FDIC chairman from 1994 to 1997, inadvertently hit upon the contradiction and dilemma: "We have a vision—the vision of an FDIC in the 21st century that continues to provide stability to the banking system by helping banks stay open to serve their customers and their communities."[3] Fine, Chairman Helfer, but what if the vision results in keeping banks open that are not economically viable in the long term? The vision then has the potential for becoming a nightmare.

The final point concerning the future of the banking industry involves its ability to cope with change. Much has been made elsewhere of data that show a declining share of the marketplace as defined by one authoritative source or another. For example, according to Federal Reserve *Flow of Funds* data, banks' share of credit market debt outstanding declined from 35 percent in 1980 to 25 percent in 1984.[4] But the focus on market share as measured by such data may be misplaced. For one thing, the simple provision of credit is only part of the financial marketplace. Financial guarantees of various sort and complex financial instruments constitute an important, and growing, component of the financial world. Banks are actively and heavily involved in the development and provision of these products and services. Evidence of the changing nature of the banking business is the increasing proportion of noninterest income in banks' operating revenues: noninterest income rose from 24.7 percent of bank net operating revenues in 1984 to 37.0 percent in 1997.[5] Another criticism of the market share approach is simply that it may be irrelevant. What seems more relevant is the banking industry's extraordinary profitability in recent years.

Although at one level market share arguments may be misleading and to an extent irrelevant, they do relate to an underlying uncertainty. The challenges posed by the seemingly increasing pace of change is an ubiquitous theme as the twentieth century gives way to the twenty first. Technological advances are fundamentally altering the way many industries do business, few more so than the banking industry. This process is not new, however. The banking industry was one of the first large-scale users of computers and for more than three decades has been largely successful in adapting to succeeding waves of innovation. Conceivably, marketplace changes or technological developments could render banks marginal, but such an occurrence seems unlikely.

An unresponsive, lethargic, static statutory and regulatory structure that hinders the banking industry's ability to respond to change is probably a greater danger to long term viability. Do the current laws and agencies constitute such a structure, not just the laws and agencies concerning banks but also those concerning the other components of the financial industry? The possibility they do should not be dismissed as remote. Individual agencies may go through periods of enlightenment regarding their own constituencies. They may, for varying lengths of time, encourage innovation and refrain from being overly protective. But rare is the agency that can take a broad perspective contrary to the apparent interests of its constituency. In other words, a balkanized regulatory structure consisting of individual agencies each concerned with protecting its own jurisdiction, and existence, might be a hindrance to broad adjustments in the financial marketplace. Thus policy-makers concerned with the big picture should be on guard against rote defenses of the status quo. By no means are all proposals for change worth implementing. But the future nature of the financial and banking industries is sufficiently uncertain to warrant a constant scrutiny of the existing legal structure, and a continuous questioning of that structure's underlying assumptions.

NOTES

1.   National Commission on Financial Institution Reform, Recovery and Enforcement, *Origins and Causes of the S&L Debacle: A Blueprint for Reform* (Washington, D.C., July 1993), p. 27.

2.   Bank Administration Institute and McKinsey & Company, Inc., *Building Better Banks: The Case for Performance-Based Regulation* (1996); The Bankers Roundtable, *Deposit Insurance Reform in the Public Interest* (1997).

3.   Helfer, Ricki, "Remarks Marking Implementation of a new Financial Information Management System for the Corporation," Arlington, Virginia, January 23, 1997.

4.   Bank Administration Institute and McKinsey & Company, Inc., pp. 11–12.

5.   Federal Deposit Insurance Corporation, *Quarterly Bank Profile*, 1st Quarter 1997. See Bank Administration Institute and McKinsey & Company, Inc., pp. 13–14, for a value-added approach to the determination of market share. Bank value-added—defined as net interest income (traditional activities) plus noninterest income (nontraditional activities)—as a percentage of gross domestic product increased from 1.0 percent in 1950 to 3.1 percent in 1993. See John H. Boyd and Mark Gertler, "Are Banks Dead? Or Are the Reports Greatly Exaggerated," *Quarterly Review*, Federal Reserve Bank of Minneapolis (Summer 1994), pp. 2–23, for a general criticism of market share analysis based on uncorrected data from the Federal Reserve's *Flow of Funds*.

Appendices

Appendix A

The Texas Banking Crash: Fate of the Ten Largest Organizations

RepublicBank Corporation ($24.2 billion in assets). Merged with InterFirst Corporation to form First Republic Bancorporation, 1987; received $1 billion loan from FDIC, March 1988; closed and bridge bank formed, July 1988; acquired by NCNB Corporation with FDIC assistance, November 1988.

MCorp ($22.6 billion in assets). Received $1 billion discount window loan, November 1988; in action precipitated by bankruptcy suit involving the holding company, 20 of 25 subsidiary banks declared insolvent by the OCC, and bridge bank formed, March 1989; acquired by Banc One of Ohio, July 1989.

InterFirst Corporation ($22.1 billion in assets). Merged with RepublicBank Corporation to form First Republic Bancorporation, 1987.

Texas Commerce Bancshares ($20.1 billion in assets). Acquired by Chemical New York Corporation, 1987.

First City Bancorporation ($16.8 billion in assets). Acquired by Robert Abboud with $970 million in FDIC open bank assistance, April 1988 (transaction announced in September 1987); 20 subsidiary banks seized by the FDIC, October 1992; acquired by Texas Commerce and others, January 1993.

Allied Bancshares ($10.2 billion in assets). Acquired by First Interstate Bancorporation of Los Angeles, California, 1987.

Texas American Bancshares ($6.4 billion in assets). FDIC readiness to aid merger with National Bancshares of Texas announced in June 1988 but transaction not consummated; closed and acquired by Deposit Guarantee Bank of Dallas, July 1989; acquired by Banc One Corporation, 1992.

Cullen/Frost Bankers ($3.3 billion in assets). Remained independent.

National Bancshares of Texas ($2.8 billion in assets). FDIC readiness to aid merger with Texas American Bancshares announced in June 1988 but transaction not consummated; FDIC open bank assistance announced in July 1989 but transaction not consummated; nine subsidiary banks closed and acquired by NCNB of Dallas, June 1990.

Banc Texas ($1.8 billion in assets). Acquired by Hallwood Group with $150 million in FDIC open bank assistance, July 1987; lead bank closed and acquired by Hibernia Corporation of Louisiana with $69 million in FDIC assistance, January 1990; financial difficulties caused Hibernia to sell its Texas banks, which included assets from BancTexas, to Comerica of Michigan, 1992.

Appendix B

The Thrift Industry in Crisis

Year	Number of Institutions	Industry Assets	Industry Net Income	Failures	Insurance Fund
1980	4,005	$620.6	$0.8	11	$6.5
1981	3,785	658.5	(4.6)	28	6.2
1982	3,349	699.5	(4.1)	63	6.3
1983	3,183	819.2	1.9	36	6.4
1984	3,136	977.5	1.0	22	5.6
1985	3,256	1,070.1	3.7	31	4.6
1986	3,220	1,163.9	0.1	46	(6.3)
1987	3,147	1,250.9	(7.8)	47	(13.7)
1988	2,949	1,350.5	(13.4)	305	(75.0)
1989	2,878	1,251.6	(6.2)	318	0.0
1990	2,521	1,084.8	(2.9)	213	0.0
1991	2,119	882.1	1.8	144	0.1
1992	1,871	806.7	5.1	59	0.3
1993	1,669	774.8	4.9	9	1.2
1994	1,543	774.1	4.3	2	1.9
1995	1,437	771.0	5.4	2	3.4
1996	1,334	769.2	4.8	1	8.9
1997	1,215	776.6	6.5	0	9.4

Notes: (1) Dollar figures in billions. (2) Institutions, assets, and net income: through 1989, FSLIC-insured institutions—U.S. League of Savings Institutions, *Savings Institutions Sourcebook*; 1990–91, number of institutions and assets—*Statistical Abstract of the United States, 1992*, FDIC, *Statistics on Banking, 1991*; 1990–91, net income, OTS-regulated institutions—OTS, *Supervising Today's Thrift Industry* (December 1992); 1992–97, OTS-regulated institutions—OTS, *Quarterly Financial Results*. (3) Failures: 1980–1988—James R. Barth, *The Great Savings and Loan Debacle* (The AEI Press, 1991), p. 32; 1989–1995—RTC, *Statistical Abstract* (8/89–9/95); 1996–97—OTS. (4) Insurance Fund: FSLIC through 1988; SAIF thereafter.

Appendix C

The Banking Industry in Trouble

Year	Number of Institutions	Industry Assets	Industry Net Income	Failures	Insurance Fund
1980	14,435	$1,855.7	$14.0	11	$11.0
1981	14,415	2,029.1	14.7	10	12.2
1982	14,451	2,193.9	14.8	42	13.8
1983	14,469	2,342.0	14.9	48	15.4
1984	14,483	2,508.9	15.5	80	16.5
1985	14,407	2.730.7	18.9	120	18.0
1986	14,199	2,940.7	17.4	145	18.3
1987	13,703	2,999.9	2.8	203	18.3
1988	13,123	3,130.8	24.8	221	14.1
1989	12,709	3,299.4	15.6	207	13.2
1990	12,343	3,389.4	16.0	169	4.0
1991	11,921	3,430.6	17.9	127	(7.0)
1992	11,462	3,506.0	32.1	122	0.0
1993	10,958	3,706.2	43.4	41	13.1
1994	10,451	4,010.5	44.7	13	21.8
1995	9,940	4,312.7	48.8	6	25.5
1996	9,528	4,578.3	52.4	5	26.9
1997	9,143	5,014.9	59.2	1	28.3

Notes: (1) Dollar figures in billions. (2) FDIC: *Historical Statistics on Banking, 1934–1992*; *Quarterly Bank Profile*, various issues; *Annual Report*, various issues.

Appendix D

Interest Rates and Inflation (%)

Year	Federal Funds Rate	Change in Consumer Price Index
1970	7.18	5.7
1971	4.66	4.4
1972	4.43	3.2
1973	8.73	6.2
1974	10.50	11.0
1975	5.82	9.1
1976	5.04	5.8
1977	5.54	6.5
1978	7.93	7.6
1979	11.19	11.3
1980	13.36	13.5
1981	16.38	10.3
1982	12.26	6.2
1983	9.09	3.2
1984	10.23	4.3
1985	8.10	3.6
1986	6.81	1.9
1987	6.66	3.6
1988	7.57	4.1
1989	9.21	4.8
1990	8.10	5.4
1991	5.69	4.2
1992	3.52	3.0
1993	3.02	3.0
1994	4.21	2.6
1995	5.83	2.8
1996	5.30	3.0
1997	5.46	2.3

Source: Economic Report of the President, February 1998, Tables B–63 and B–73.

Appendix E

Major Banking Laws, 1980–1996

1980   Depository Institutions Deregulation and Monetary Control Act (DIDMCA). Established the Depository Institutions Deregulation Committee and provided for the phasing out of interest rate ceilings. Extended nationwide the authority of depository institutions to issue NOW accounts or their equivalent. Required all depository institutions offering transaction accounts to maintain reserves with the Federal Reserve System. Expanded the powers of federal S&Ls. Raised the federal deposit insurance limit from $40,000 to $100,000. Pub. L. 96–221.

1982   Garn-St Germain Depository Institutions Act. Its most notable provisions authorized interstate emergency mergers and acquisitions and expanded the powers of federal S&Ls and savings banks. Pub. L. 97–320.

Title I, the Deposit Insurance Flexibility Act, expanded the FDIC's power to assist troubled banks, authorized certain acquisitions on an interstate or cross-industry basis, allowed the FHLBB to charter savings banks that retained their FDIC insurance, and permitted the FDIC to convert a state mutual savings bank into a federal stock savings bank under certain circumstances.

Title II, the Net Worth Certificate Act, authorized the FDIC and the FHLBB to provide capital assistance through the purchase, with promissory notes, of net worth certificates.

Title III expanded the powers of federal S&Ls and savings banks.

Title IV increased the lending limit for national banks and made a number of changes regarding insider transactions.

Title V restricted the insurance activities of bank holding companies.

Title VI made a number of changes in the Federal Credit Union Act to give credit unions greater flexibility and authority in daily operations.

Title VII allowed financial institutions to offer NOW accounts and share draft accounts to state and local governments, directed certain studies be made regarding deposit insurance, and expanded the powers of bank service corporations.

1983   International Lending Supervision Act. Imposed controls over the international lending activities of U.S. banking organizations. Directed the federal banking agencies to establish minimum capital levels. Pub. L. 98–181, Title IX. 12 U.S.C. §§3901–3912.

1987   Competitive Equality Banking Act (CEBA). A 12-title law that, among other things, addressed certain inequities among depository institutions and attempted to deal with the escalating S&L crisis. Pub. L. 100–86.

Title I, the Competitive Equality Amendments of 1987, prohibited the establishment of new "nonbank banks," imposed certain restrictions on existing "nonbank banks" and their parent organizations, and created the concept of a "qualified thrift lender," a definition that had to be met if an organization wanted to enjoy certain benefits of being a thrift.

Title II imposed a temporary moratorium on Federal agency approvals of certain securities, insurance, and real estate activities by banks, bank holding companies, and foreign banks.

Title III was a plan to recapitalize the FSLIC in the amount of $10.8 billion.

Title IV, the Thrift Industry Recovery Act, mandated the adoption by the FHLBB and the FSLIC of regulations concerning accounting, appraisal, reserve, and capital standards. A forbearance program for certain weak thrifts was also to be instituted.

Title V extended, with modifications, the emergency interstate acquisition provisions of the Garn-St Germain Act of 1982, authorized the FDIC to establish "bridge banks" to aid in arranging mergers or other disposition transactions for failing banks, and extended Garn-St Germain's new worth certificate program for five years.

Title VI, the Expedited Funds Availability Act, limited the number of days a depository institution could restrict the availability of funds deposited in any transaction account.

Title VII made a number of changes in the Federal Credit Union Act.

Title VIII authorized agriculturally oriented banks to amortize loan losses over an extended period of time.

Title IX provided that federally insured deposits were backed by the full faith and credit of the government.

Titles X–XII concerned certain miscellaneous matters and mandated various studies.

1989   Financial Institutions Reform, Recovery, and Enforcement Act (FIRREA). A 14-title law that established the Resolution Trust Corporation to manage and resolve failed savings institutions; abolished the FHLBB and the FSLIC; created the Office of Thrift Supervision within the Treasury Department to replace the FHLBB; and created the Savings Association Insurance Fund under the control of the FDIC to replace the FSLIC. Pub. L. 101–73.

Title I set forth the act's purposes.

Title II renamed the FDIC's existing fund as the Bank Insurance Fund (BIF); created a second fund—the Savings Association Insurance Fund (SAIF)—under the FDIC's jurisdiction; set forth assessment and funding instructions for the funds; gave the FDIC resolution powers concerning failed or failing SAIF–insured thrifts; established cross–guarantee liability for commonly controlled depository institutions; gave the FDIC the power to restrict the acquisition of brokered deposits by troubled institutions; imposed certain limitations on the powers of state–chartered thrifts; and prohibited investments by thrifts in junk bonds.

Title III created the OTS; mandated that thrift capital standards be at least as stringent as capital standards for national banks; strengthened the qualified thrift lender test; added an additional restriction on thrift commercial real estate loans of 400 percent of capital; and required thrifts to adhere to national bank standards regarding limits on loans to one borrower and transactions with affiliates.

Title IV abolished the FHLBB and the FSLIC and provided for the transfer of their functions.

Title V created the RTC and authorized $50 billion for the S&L cleanup. The RTC was to resolve all formerly FSLIC-insured institutions failing between January 1, 1989, and August 9, 1992. The RTC was to cease to exist on December 31, 1996.

Title VI amended the Bank Holding Company Act, giving the Federal Reserve Board the specific authority to permit bank holding companies to acquire thrifts.

Title VII made a number of changes in the organization and operation of the Federal Home Loan Bank System, including the creation of the Federal Housing Finance Board to oversee the Federal Home Loan Banks.

Title VIII granted to the Comptroller of the Currency clearer powers to appoint conservators for national banks.

Title IX expanded and strengthened enforcement powers.

Title X mandated several studies, including a Treasury Department–coordinated study of the deposit insurance system.

Title XI provided for regulation of the real estate appraisal industry.

Titles XII–XIV dealt with a number of topics, including taxes and additional studies.

1990   Assessment Rates—the Omnibus Budget Reconciliation Act removed caps on assessment rate increases and allowed for semiannual rate increases. 12 U.S.C. §1817(b). It also permitted the FDIC, on behalf of the BIF and the SAIF, to borrow from the Federal Financing Bank (FFB) on terms and conditions determined by the FFB. 12 U.S.C. §1824(b). Pub. L. 101–508.

Comprehensive Thrift and Bank Fraud Prosecution and Taxpayer Recovery Act—Title XXV of the Crime Control Act of 1990. Contained a variety of provisions designed to assist the FDIC and the RTC in preventing and punishing fraud in the banking and thrift industries. Gave the FDIC and the RTC the authority to ask a court to freeze the assets of persons who defraud depository institutions. Prevents individuals who defraud financial institutions from using the federal bankruptcy code to discharge debts or shield assets. Authorized the FDIC to prohibit excessive bonuses, benefits, and "golden parachute" severance packages for departing officers, directors, and employees of troubled institutions. For codification, see 12 U.S.C. §1001 note. Pub. L. 101–647.

Subtitle F established a National Commission on Financial Institution Reform, Recovery, and Enforcement to examine the origin and causes of the thrift crisis and to make recommendations on preventing recurrences.

Subtitle H, the Financial Institutions Anti-Fraud Enforcement Act of 1990, encouraged private persons to inform the government of violations that could give rise to civil penalties and of specific assets that could be recovered in satisfaction of judgments. 12 U.S.C. §§4201–4247.

1991   Resolution Trust Corporation Funding Act. Provided an additional $30 billion for the S&L cleanup. Pub. L. 102–18.

Resolution Trust Corporation Refinancing, Restructuring and Improvement Act.

Provided an additional $25 billion for the S&L cleanup; extended the ending date for the period during which failed thrifts became the responsibility of the RTC from August 9, 1992, to September 30, 1993; made changes in the control structure of the RTC; and relaxed the real estate appraisal requirements of the FIRREA. Pub. L. 102–233.

Title III, the Resolution Trust Corporation Thrift Depositor Protection Reform Act, replaced the RTC Oversight Board with the less powerful and intrusive Thrift Depositor Protection Oversight Board, abolished the RTC Board of Directors (which had been the FDIC Board of Directors wearing a different hat), and replaced the FDIC as manager of the RTC with the chief executive officer of the RTC.

Federal Deposit Insurance Corporation Improvement Act (FDICIA). Provided for recapitalization of the FDIC's Bank Insurance Fund, and tightened regulation and supervision of banks and thrifts in a number of areas. The regulatory and supervisory changes included (1) creation of five capital-to-assets ratio categories and articulation of detailed actions to be taken by bank supervisors if an institution's capital declines (prompt corrective action); (2) requirement that banks and thrifts be examined and audited annually; (3) establishment of a least-cost standard to be followed by the FDIC in resolving failing institutions; (4) prohibition on use of brokered deposits by low capitalized institutions; (5) requirement that the FDIC institute a risk-based assessment system for deposit insurance assessments; (6) restrictions on the activities of state banks; and (7) requirement that the banking agencies promulgate standards concerning real estate lending, operational and managerial matters, asset quality, earnings, stock valuation, and compensation. Pub. L. 102–242.

Title II, Subtitle A, the Foreign Bank Supervision Enhancement Act, strengthened the regulation and supervision of foreign banks.

Title II, Subtitle C, the Bank Enterprise Act, provided for reduced insurance assessment rates for lifeline accounts and assessment credits for lending and other activities in distressed areas.

Title II, Subtitle F, the Truth in Savings Act, required adequate disclosure of terms and conditions about interest on savings vehicles.

Title IV, Subtitle G, the Qualified Thrift Lender Reform Act, relaxed the qualified thrift lender test for thrifts.

1992   Regulatory Burden—The Housing and Community Development Act contained a number of provisions relaxing statutory requirements on depository institutions. Among other things, the act prohibited the FDIC from setting a specific range of compensation for officers, directors, and employees of insured financial institutions. 12 U.S.C. §1831p–1(d). Pub. L. 102–550.

1993   Depositor Preference. Title III, §3001, of the Omnibus Budget Reconciliation Act amended the FDI Act to give depositors a preference over general creditors and shareholders when a receiver distributes assets from failed banks and thrifts. Because the FDIC is subrogated to the claims of insured depositors, the amendment increased the FDIC's share of the recoveries of the assets of failed institutions. Pub. L. 103–66. 12 U.S.C. §1821(d)(11).

Resolution Trust Corporation Completion Act. Released to the RTC up to $18.1 billion in previously authorized funding that had lapsed April 1, 1992. Changed the date on which the RTC was scheduled to terminate from December 31, 1996, to December 31, 1995. Extended the RTC's authority to be appointed conservator or receiver of failed thrifts from September 30, 1993, to a date between January 1, 1995, and July 1, 1995, the exact date to be selected by the chairperson of the Thrift Depositor Protection Oversight Board. Established transitional procedures for the folding of the RTC back into the FDIC. Established a new SAIF funding schedule, reducing the maximum authorization of appropriations from the FIRREA's $32 billion to $8 billion. Specified certain management and operational reforms for the FDIC and the RTC. Pub. L. 103–204.

1994   Riegle Community Development and Regulatory Improvement Act. A five-title law that, among other things, authorized financial assistance for community development financial institutions and scaled back the regulatory burden on federally regulated banks and thrifts. Pub. L. 103–325.

Title I, Subtitle A, the Community Development Banking and Financial Institutions Act, created a community development fund and authorized it to provide financial and technical assistance to Community Development Financial Institutions (CDFIs). Any entity, including an insured depository institution, may seek qualification as a CDFI.

Title I, Subtitle B, the Home Ownership and Equity Protection Act, established disclosure requirements and standards concerning home equity lending.

Title II, Subtitle A, the Small Business Loan Securitization and Secondary Market Enhancement Act, built on the framework for securitization established by the Secondary Mortgage Market Enhancement Act of 1984 by creating a similar framework for small business-related securities.

Title II, Subtitle B, established a Small Business Capital Enhancement Program to assist in providing access to debt capital for small business concerns.

Title III contained a number of provisions designed to reduce regulatory burden.

Title IV, the Money Laundering Suppression Act, imposed requirements on the Secretary of the Treasury and the banking agencies designed to better control money laundering.

Title V, the National Flood Insurance Reform Act, expanded flood insurance purchase requirements and mandated that the banking agencies and the National Credit Union Administration ensure compliance on the part of depository institutions.

Riegle–Neal Interstate Banking and Branching Efficiency Act. Authorized banks, beginning June 1, 1997, to branch across state lines through merger. States could accelerate the effective date and can allow de novo branching. States could also opt out of interstate branching altogether if they did so by June 1, 1997. Authorized bank holding companies beginning one year after enactment to acquire banks located in any state. Pub. L. 103–328.

1996   Small Business Job Protection Act. Section 1616 repealed the provision of the IRC, Section 593, authorizing the reserve method of accounting for bad debts by thrift institutions. The section also forgave the recapture of bad debt reserves for taxable years before 1988, thus removing a financial barrier to the conversion of thrifts to banks. Pub. L. 104–188.

Economic Growth and Regulatory Paperwork Reduction Act. Contained a number of regulatory relief measures, including imposition of a 60–day time period for the FDIC's consideration of a state bank application to engage in an activity not permissible for a national bank; removal of ATMs from branch closure notification requirements; and exemption of certain other branch closures from notification requirements. Mandated that one of the public members of the FDIC board have state bank supervisory experience. Excluded retirement certificates of deposit from the definition of "deposit," thus making them ineligible for deposit insurance coverage. Pub. L. 104–208.

Subtitle G, the Deposit Insurance Funds Act, provided for capitalization of the Savings Association Insurance Fund and for the spreading of the FICO (Financing Corporation) obligation to include banks. The SAIF was to be capitalized at the designated reserve ratio of 1.25 percent of insured deposits through a special assessment on SAIF members. Full pro rata responsibility of banks for FICO assessments was to be in place by December 31, 1999, or the date on which the last savings association ceased to exist if earlier. Prior to that time, banks were to make FICO payments at one–fifth the rate imposed on SAIF–insured institutions. The BIF and the SAIF were to be merged on January 1, 1999, if no savings association existed on that date. The Treasury was to study the development of a common charter and report to Congress by March 31, 1997.

Selected Bibliography

Akhtar, M. A. "Causes and Consequences of the 1989–92 Credit Slowdown: Overview and Perspective." *Federal Reserve Bank of New York Quarterly Review* (Winter 1993–94).

Bank Administration Institute and McKinsey & Company, Inc. *Building Better Banks: The Case for Performance-Based Regulation.* 1996.

The Bankers Roundtable. *Deposit Insurance Reform in the Public Interest.* 1997.

Barth, James R. *The Great Savings and Loan Debacle.* Washington, D.C.: The AEI Press, 1991.

Bernanke, Ben S. "Credit in the Macroeconomy." *Federal Reserve Bank of New York Quarterly Review* (Spring 1993).

Board of Governors of the Federal Reserve System. *Guide to the Flow of Funds Accounts.* 1993.

Cantor, Richard, and John Wenninger. "Perspective on the Credit Slowdown." *Federal Reserve Bank of New York Quarterly Review* (Spring 1993).

Chapman, John M., and Ray B. Westerfield. *Branch Banking: Its Historical and Theoretical Position in America and Abroad.* New York and London: Harper & Brothers Publishers, 1942.

Corrigan, E. Gerald. "The Banking-Commerce Controversy Revisited." *Quarterly Review*, Federal Reserve Bank of New York (Spring 1991, Vol. 16/1).

De Long, J. Bradford. "What Morgan Wrought." *The Wilson Quarterly* (Autumn 1992).

Department of Commerce. *Historical Statistics of the United States, Colonial Times to 1970.* Washington, D.C.: U.S. Government Printing Office.

Dunham, Constance. "The Growth of Money Market Funds." *New England Economic Review*, Federal Reserve Bank of Boston (September–October 1980).

Federal Deposit Insurance Corporation. *Annual Reports.*

_____. *Historical Statistics on Banking,* various years.

_____. *History of the Eighties; Lessons for the Future.* 1997.

_____. *Mandate for Change.* 1987.

_____. *Statistics on Banking,* various years.

Federal Reserve Bank of New York. *Studies on Causes and Consequences of the 1989–92 Credit Slowdown.* 1993.

_____. *Studies on Excess Capacity in the Financial Sector.* June 1993.

Federal Reserve Bank of Dallas. *1984 Annual Report.*

Fein, Melanie L., and M. Michele Faber. "The Separation of Banking and Commerce in American Banking History." An Appendix to a Statement by Federal Reserve Board Chairman Paul Volcker before a subcommittee of the House Committee on Government

Operations, June 11, 1986.

Fissel, Gary S. "The Anatomy of the LDC Debt Crisis." *FDIC Banking Review* (Spring/Summer 1991, Vol. 4, No. 1).

Frydl, Edward J. "Overhangs and Hangovers: Coping with the Imbalances of the 1980s." *Annual Report 1991*, Federal Reserve Bank of New York.

General Accounting Office. *Financial Audit: Resolution Trust Corporation's 1995 and 1994 Financial Statements.*, GAO/AIMD-96-123, 1996.

Golembe, Carter H. "The Deposit Insurance Legislation of 1933." *Political Science Quarterly* (June 1960, Vol. 67).

_____. " 'Hold That Line'—The Federal Reserve Board's View of the Banking Business." *Golembe Reports* (Vol. 1986–8).

_____. "A Thanksgiving Basket—Mr. Boesky; FDIC/FSLIC; the Number of Commercial Banks; Banking and Commerce Revisited." *Golembe Reports* (Vol. 1986–10).

Grant, James. *Money of the Mind.* New York: Farrar, Straus & Giroux, 1992.

Grant, Joseph M. *The Great Texas Banking Crash; An Insider's Account.* Austin: University of Texas Press, 1996.

Holland, David, Don Inscoe, Ross Waldrop, and William Kuta. "Interstate Banking— The Past, Present, and Future." *FDIC Banking Review* (Fall 1996, Vol. 9, No. 1).

Kindlebeger, Charles P. *Manias, Panics, and Crashes: A History of Financial Crises.* New York: Basic Books, 1978.

Kovacevich, Richard M., "Deposit Insurance: It's Time to Cage the Monster." *Banking Policy Report* (November 20, 1995).

McKelvey, Edward F. "Interest Rate Ceilings and Disintermediation." *Staff Economic Studies*, No. 99, Board of Governors of the Federal Reserve System (April 1978).

Mester, Loretta J. "Banking and Commerce: A Dangerous Liaison?" *Business Review*, Federal Reserve Bank of Philadelphia (May–June 1992).

Moyer, R. Charles, and Robert E. Lamy. " 'Too Big to Fail': Rationale, Consequences, and Alternatives." *Business Economics* (July 1992).

National Commission on Financial Institution Reform, Recovery and Enforcement. *Origins and Causes of the S&L Debacle: A Blueprint for Reform.* Washington, D.C., July 1993.

O'Keefe, John. "The Texas Banking Crisis: Causes and Consequences, 1980–1989." *FDIC Banking Review* (Winter 1990, Vol. 3, No. 2).

Robertson, Ross M., updated by Jesse M. Stiller. *The Comptroller and Bank Supervision*, 2d ed. Washington, D.C.: Office of the Comptroller of the Currency, 1995.

Rosine, John, and Nicholas Walraven. "Drought, Agriculture, and the Economy." *Federal Reserve Bulletin* (January 1989).

Seidman, L. William. *Full Faith and Credit.* New York: Times Books, 1995.

Sprague, Irvine H. *Bailout.* New York: Basic Books, Inc., 1986.

Yergen, Daniel. *The Prize.* New York: Simon & Schuster, 1991.

Index

About the Author

DAVID S. HOLLAND has been a bank consultant and an editor of a financial industry newsletter. Currently, he is an analyst with the Federal Deposit Insurance Corporation. Dr. Holland has written extensively, with articles in such journals as *The Golembe Reports* and *FDIC Banking Review*.

ISBN 0-275-96356-X

HARDCOVER BAR CODE